WILLIAM BENDIX IN DETROIT PRODUCTION OF "GENERAL SEEGER."

PHOTO BY FRIEDMAN-ABELES

GENERAL
SEEGER

BY IRA LEVIN

DRAMATISTS
PLAY SERVICE
INC.

To

FLORA ROBERTS

GENERAL SEEGER was presented by the Theatre of Michigan Company and Theodore Mann at the Lyceum Theatre in New York City on February 28, 1962. It was staged by George C. Scott; lighting was by Ralph Holmes; costumes by Noel Taylor; and setting by Gerald Parker. The cast, in order of appearance, was as follows:

A CORPORAL ....Roscoe Lee Browne

A WOMAN ....Dolores Sutton

CAPTAIN PECK ....Gerald Richards

CAPTAIN THIBAUDEAU ....Paul Stevens

LT. COLONEL BONNEY ....Lonny Chapman

MAJOR GENERAL VOHS ....John Leslie

BOYD McKAY ....Tim O'Connor

MAJOR GENERAL SEEGER ....George C. Scott

RENA SEEGER ....Ann Harding

REPORTERS, PHOTOGRAPHERS
Charles Dierkop, J. Nathan French, Elaine Hyman, John O'Leary, Loree Marks, Thomas Maxwell, Martin Priest, Tom Signorelli, Frank Simpson

COLOR GUARDS ....Johnny Cosgrove, Matt Bennett

CHARACTERS

A CORPORAL

A WOMAN

CAPTAIN PECK

CAPTAIN THIBAUDEAU

LIEUTENANT COLONEL BONNEY

MAJOR GENERAL VOHS

BOYD MCKAY

MAJOR GENERAL SEEGER
RENA SEEGER

REPORTERS

PHOTOGRAPHERS

A PRIVATE

The action takes place on an Army post in one of the
New England states, in the office of the Commanding
General. The time is peacetime; a Saturday in a recent
July.

There are two acts.

The characters in this play, including those who hold existing
military or civilian offices, are fictional and not intended to represent
specific persons, living or dead.

Occasional minor license has been taken with military procedure and
terminology.

I. L.

SETTING

An Army post in one of the New England states. The Commanding General's office and a portion of the anteroom.

A cyclorama. U. C., a broad walnut executive desk with occupant's and visitor's chairs of maroon leather. An American flag stands U. L. of the desk; a red flag with two white stars (the official flag of a Major General) stands U. R. of it. Suspended in space behind the occupant's chair hangs a large gilt-framed painting of a hearty young Army lieutenant standing at ease and smiling directly into the eyes of the observer. The top of the portrait hangs higher than the eagles of the flanking flags.

The imaginary R. wall of the office is marked by a free-standing window and, farther D., a maroon leather couch flanked by ashstands. The window has a Venetian blind, blue drapes, and an air-conditioning unit mounted in its lower section. The imaginary L. wall of the office is marked by a free-standing pair of walnut double doors and, farther D., a slat-backed chair and a walnut table. The double doors, which open outward, are symmetrically opposed to the window unit at R. There should be two or three chairs in addition to those already mentioned.

The anteroom section is at extreme L., quite narrow. Adjacent to the slat-backed chair and walnut table (on the other side of the imaginary wall) stands a small secretarial desk, facing U. Below it, a posture-back swivel chair. The imaginary L. wall of the anteroom is marked by a free-standing single door which opens inward and, D., a visitors' settee and a gray steel filing cabinet.

There is a telephone on the secretarial desk and two on the executive desk, although only one is used in the course of the play.

* * *

GENERAL SEEGER

ACT I

SCENE: *Darkness and silence. Out of the distance, faintly, comes the sound of a field drum, rat-a-tat-tatting a half-time marching cadence. It grows louder, approaching, and louder still, reverberant, tightening the bearer's stomach, and then it turns away, fading into the distance again . . .*
AT RISE: *The curtain rises slowly. The set stands empty against the bright summer blueness of the cyclorama. The window blind is closed, a shaft of sunlight strikes against it from the wings and filters through to suffuse the office with a limpid morning half-light. The double doors to the anteroom are opened, the single anteroom door is closed. The drum dies out. The single door opens and a Corporal enters. He is 24. About his left arm is pinned a white cloth band with the initials P.J.O. stencilled in black. He carries his cap and a clip-board filled with varicolored papers. Seeing that no one is about, he walks into the office. He stands for a moment, fanning himself once or twice with the clip-board, and then goes to the window and studies the controls of the air-conditioning unit. He turns it on, adjusts it, feels the air-flow. He opens the blind and glances at what lies below, squinting against the sunlight. Then he turns, comes D. and addresses the audience.*

CORPORAL. Welcome to the theatre, ladies and gentlemen. The name of the play is *General Seeger*. Seeger, please; not *SeeGAR*. (*Tucks his cap into his belt.*) A number of years ago my trick knee maliciously untricked itself and I was drafted into the Army. The most recent war had ended, and so, after Basic Training and a few improbable months at Radar School, I found myself at Fort Name-

7

less, in one of the New England states, a corporal attached to the Public Information Office. (*Indicates his armband.*) The P.I.O. This armband, by the way, is my own handiwork. I'm quite proud of its official appearance. If you know a boy who's been drafted, tell him to make an armband. Sergeants fall back in awe, lieutenants are disquieted, even captains and majors talk gently to the man with an armband. Any initials; it makes no difference. This is the Commanding General's office, on the second floor of Headquarters Building. It's twenty past ten on Saturday morning, July twelfth, and throughout the post those without armbands are readying themselves for a parade. High brass has come here today, to attend the dedication of a shiny new building. It stands at the far end of the post, near the barracks where the trainees are billeted. It's a recreation center for the enlisted men, and a beautiful one, although it kills me to admit it. There are two lounges, a cafeteria, a library, a music room, a gymnasium, and a blue Olympic swimming pool, all housed under a flying wing of white concrete miraculously poised on vertical sheets of pale green glass. That sterling description comes easy; we chaps in P.I.O. have sent it out this week to every newspaper and magazine from Abbeville, Alabama, to Zion, Illinois. In peacetime, in a democracy, an army travels, not on its stomach, but on its favorable publicity. And so . . . at three this afternoon, Himself, Our Leader— (*A gesture at the desk behind him.*)—Major General William J. Seeger, known to the troops as Eager-Seeger or Cigar Butt, will unveil a bronze plaque mounted on the portal of the new recreation center. An element of human interest creeps in at this point, and constitutes the real reason reporters and photographers have come here today; for the building is to be dedicated, not to some unrelated hero of long-ago battles, but to a man much—

WOMAN. (*Cutting in on "battles."*) Excuse me. (*A woman is standing in the double doorway. She is in her early thirties, slim, neatly dressed, tense. She carries a purse and a small blue satchel with a white wing printed on it.*) Is this General Seeger's office?

CORPORAL. Yes, ma'am.

WOMAN. He isn't here?

CORPORAL. No, ma'am. Are you a reporter?

WOMAN. No, I'm—not.

CORPORAL. The General will be here in ten minutes or so. Would you like to wait?

WOMAN. (*Retreating toward visitors' settee.*) Yes. Thank you. I'll wait . . .

CORPORAL. You can sit in here if you'd like. The air-conditioning doesn't make it out there.

WOMAN. Oh, thank you. (*Entering office uncertainly.*) It's terribly hot, isn't it?

CORPORAL. Ninety-two, and still rising. (*To the audience.*) Here is the play, ladies and gentlemen. This woman begins it.

WOMAN. It's supposed to go up past ninety-five . . . (*Before the desk, she stands looking up at the portrait behind it. Corporal moves u.*)

CORPORAL. That's the General's son. A first lieutenant. He's dead now.

WOMAN. He smiled as though he intended to live forever. . . .

CORPORAL. Thirty-one years . . . The new building today is being dedicated in his honor. He gave his life to save a couple of lame-brained enlisted men.

WOMAN. (*Moving away R.*) Are you the General's orderly?

CORPORAL. No, I'm with the Public Information Office. Have you an appointment with the General?

WOMAN. No, I haven't. He knows me, though. He'll see me. (*She sits on the couch D. R., putting her purse and satchel beside her. Corporal has observed her tension, studies her. She feels his eyes.*) Is this building always so deathly quiet?

CORPORAL. Saturday isn't a regular duty day.

WOMAN. (*An ill-at-ease pause.*) If you have any work to take care of, please don't let me interfere.

CORPORAL. (*Crosses u. to R. of desk.*) I'm just waiting for the chief of my office. We have a press meeting here in a few minutes.

WOMAN. (*With a caustic edge.*) And the General will make a little speech to the reporters.

CORPORAL. (*Registering her inflection. Sits on back of chair, D. R. of desk.*) Yes, ma'am. Judging from that bag, you came here by airplane.

WOMAN. (*Studying her R. hand.*) Corporal, may I ask you a hypothetical question?

CORPORAL. Yes, ma'am.

WOMAN. (*With a forced flippancy.*) My hands, you have noticed no doubt, are trembling. If I were to take a small bottle of whiskey from this bag and draw off, say, a quarter-inch of its contents, would you think me—an alcoholic?

CORPORAL. (*Pause.*) Maybe. Or you might be a woman under some . . . unusual tension, for whom a drink would be . . . wise medicine. I don't think I'd form a fixed opinion either way.

WOMAN. That's fair enough, Corporal. . . . Let's make the question *un*-hypothetical . . . (*Unzips satchel and takes out a pint bottle with a cap that serves as a drinking cup.*)

CORPORAL. (*Starting* L.) I'll get a glass.

WOMAN. (*Stopping him at* C.) Don't bother; the top of the bottle does the trick. (*Pouring.*) This is a Saint Christopher's bottle; the patron saint of travelers. (*Holding up bottle.*) You see? It's almost full. If I were an alcoholic it would be almost empty, wouldn't it? I bought it yesterday afternoon.

CORPORAL. (*Smiling.*) You're not an alcoholic.

WOMAN. (*She looks at him.*) Thank you. I don't want to be. (*Sips, then offers bottle.*) Are you?

CORPORAL. No. No, thanks. (*Woman sips again. Corporal moves* R. *to window, watches her from this new perspective.*) Have you traveled far?

WOMAN. From San Francisco to New York, from New York to Boston, from Boston to here.

CORPORAL. To see the ceremonies today?

WOMAN. No, I've seen enough of military ceremonies. They leave me quite cold. In fact you might say they freeze me to death. (*She sips again.*)

CORPORAL. (*Crossing* D. *of chair* D. R. *of desk.*) You flew all this way just to see the General?

WOMAN. Yes. (*Caps the bottle, her tension not visibly diminished.*)

CORPORAL. You're a relative of his?

WOMAN. Everything you say is a question, Corporal. (*She puts bottle in satchel, zips it closed. Voices are heard off* L.)

CORPORAL. I'm sorry. I didn't mean to be rude.

WOMAN. It's all right. You weren't, really. People are coming. (*Corporal moves to* C.) Let me stay in here, please. (*Corporal looks at her for a moment. She meets his gaze effortfully. He turns to doorway and then to audience.*)

CORPORAL. Captain Peck, the chief of the Public Information Office, followed by reporters and photographers. (*Captain Peck*

10

*enters, the professional greeter's smile lingering on his face. He is
36, likeable, a bit hasty and nervous on this special day.)*

PECK. Ah, here you are.

CORPORAL. Morning, sir.

PECK. Do you have all the info sheets? *(Corporal shows clip-
board in answer.)* Good. *(The first of the reporters and photographers are entering.)* Right in here, gentlemen, ladies . . . *(Seeing
the woman.)* Are you with the press, Miss?

WOMAN. *(Taking cigarette from purse.)* No, I'm not.

PECK. *(Turning quickly to door.)* Come right in! I'm afraid there
aren't going to be enough seats. Quite frankly, we weren't expecting such a fine turn-out! *(Reporters and photographers enter. There
are seven or eight in all, two of them women. Two of the men
carry cameras. Some of them take seats immediately, others drift
about the room.)*

FIRST REPORTER. *(A woman, indicating portrait.)* Isn't this
Lieutenant Seeger?

PECK. Yes. Yes, it is.

SECOND REPORTER. *(A man, looking out window. To another
reporter near him.)* I'll tell you, I'd just as soon watch the parade
from up here.

THIRD REPORTER. Can we take any seats?

PECK. *(Indicating seats near desk.)* Well, I think we'd better leave
those . . .

FIRST REPORTER. *(To the woman.)* May I?

WOMAN. Oh, yes. *(Woman takes her satchel and purse from
couch, puts satchel on floor D. R. First reporter sits next to woman.)*
SECOND REPORTER. *(Still at window.)* Will we be out in the
sun or do we get to sit under the awning there?

PECK. Oh, you'll be under the awning. All the guests . . .

FOURTH REPORTER. Is that Lieutenant Seeger? *(Corporal has
gone L. into anteroom and now brings swivel chair into office, offer-
ing it to a reporter near door.)*

PECK. Yes, it is. Please, if you'll all take whatever seats you can
find . . . Leaving those, please. We're only going to be here for
a few minutes. I'm sorry there aren't enough seats for all of you,
but quite frankly we weren't expecting such a fine turnout. *(Reporters and photographers have now grouped themselves about the
office; most sitting, a few standing, one sitting on U. arm of couch.
Corporal is crouching on his haunches D. L. Peck stands C. Woman*

11

is smoking, as are a few of the reporters.) Now, then . . . The Corporal here has some information sheets that he's going to give you. (*Corporal rises and begins distributing typed and stapled papers to the reporters. Peck glances at a card he holds in his palm.*) These sheets contain a little data on General Seeger and our special guests, including official titles and correct spelling of names. The sheets also include some interesting facts and figures on the Recreation Center and a short biography of *Lieutenant* Seeger. Now . . . there is one change. One of our special guests, Lieutenant General Del Ruth, the First Army Commander, is unable to be here today. To represent him he has sent Major General Ernest C. Vohs—that's V-O-H-S; Vohs—whose official title is Deputy Commanding General of the First Army. (*Several reporters are jotting this down.*) Deputy . . . Commanding General . . . of the First Army . . . (*Corporal has just given information sheets to first reporter and is crossing* L., *away from couch.*)

WOMAN. May I have one of those? (*Corporal turns, hesitates a beat, crosses* R. *and gives woman information sheets.*)

SECOND REPORTER. Why did General Del Ruth cancel?

WOMAN. Thank you.

PECK. I honestly don't know. He just sent a wire saying he couldn't make it and that Vohs was coming instead. Duties, I suppose. (*During the following, woman studies information sheets and Corporal resumes his crouching position* D. L.) Now as I said, we'll only be in here a few minutes. General Seeger will introduce you to our special guests, and he also wanted the chance to say a few informal words to you before the official proceedings begin. The parade will take place in half an hour on the field down below; that's eleven o'clock. The luncheon is twelve to two-thirty at the Officers Club—there'll be cars to transport you—and the dedication of the Recreation Center will begin promptly at three and should only take fifteen or twenty minutes. Afterwards there'll be a tour of the building. (*Another reference to his notes.*) Oh, one final point. This meeting here is informal, as I said, and General Seeger has asked that there be no taking of photographs. You can take all the pictures you want later in the day, and our own photographers' prints will also be made available to you. (*Glances at his watch, then off* L.) Let's see now . . . If any of you, after touring the Recreation Center, should want to visit other parts of the post—the Ordnance School or the training battalions—we'll be more than happy to— Ah! (*Captain Thibaudeau has entered quickly during the final words of the above. He nods at Peck from the doorway and exits again.*) That was General Seeger's aide. They're coming now. Gentlemen, ladies . . . (*Everyone rises except the woman. She folds her information sheets precisely. Others face the doorway. Boyd McKay, Major General Vohs, Lieutenant Colonel Bonney, Major General Seeger, Rena Seeger and Captain Thibaudeau enter. They group themselves before the desk. Thibaudeau remaining U. L. Cyclorama has become a warm yellow-gold.*) Ladies and gentlemen: General Seeger. General: the reporters. (*Peck steps aside U. R.*)

SEEGER. Thank you, Captain. And thank you all for coming here today. I am so—very, very pleased . . . Sit down, please. Sit . . . (*Reporters and photographers who were sitting resume their seats. Seeger watches them, flushed with pride and happiness impossible for him to conceal. He is 57, a strong, forceful man. The woman, at the D. end of the couch, is sitting turned well toward the front, partially shielding her face with the folded information sheets in her U. hand.*) I'd like to introduce three honored visitors. This is Mr. Boyd McKay, ladies and gentlemen, the Assistant Secretary of the Army. (*McKay nods, smiles. He is in his early fifties, immaculately dressed, cool, reserved.*) And Major General Vohs, the Deputy Commanding General of the First Army. . . . (*Vohs is in his late fifties, white-haired, warm, with an air of judicial dignity.*) Lieutenant Colonel Bonney, of the Weapons Testing Center at Fort Colleran, Oklahoma. Colonel Bonney was Lieutenant Seeger's senior officer at the time of his death. (*Bonney is in his mid-forties, looking more like a doctor than a military man. There is a faint aura of unease about him.*) And this is my wife, ladies and gentlemen.

RENA. Thank you all for coming here . . . (*Rena is 54, nervous, anxious-eyed. She is trying to appear as happy as Seeger, but she is not. Her eyes seldom leave him.*)

SEEGER. Gentlemen, would you sit for a minute or two, please? I want to say something to these people, and to you, too. (*McKay, Vohs and Bonney take seats. Rena looks about uncertainly. Thibaudeau moves a chair toward her; she takes it gratefully. Seeger, before the desk, waits until all are settled. A feeling of gravity clouds over his earlier exuberance.*) This afternoon I'm going to make a formal speech dedicating our new Recreation Center to the memory of First Lieutenant William J. Seeger, Junior, and when I

13

do, I'm not going to say anything at all about Lieutenant Seeger being my son. A military ceremony isn't the place for bringing up personal relationships. Higher authorities put me in command of this post, and a building went up, and now higher authorities have decided who gets the honor of the dedication; *personal* relationships are—irrelevant. It wouldn't be honest, though, for me to go through the whole day pretending that the relationship didn't exist, because today of all days it's—very much in my mind, and I know it's in some of your minds, too. So I want to say a few words now *informally*; not as Commanding General Seeger, just as Lieutenant Bill Seeger's father. It's a—terrible thing when a man lives longer than his own son. It's—backwards, reversed. You expect a son to go on beyond you. You give him your name, junior . . . it's as if you're trying to make a *chain*. And when the link you put forward in front of you gets broken, well—that's the end of the chain, right there. When the son dies, the father dies, too. All right. It's sad. But we've each got a death coming to us sooner or later, and the finest way a man can meet his death, it seems to me, isn't to be ambushed by it, to have it spring out at him from an accident or an illness. No, the finest way is to face it squarely, with awareness, for a purpose. To die *for* something instead of to die *of* something. Bill saw those two boys in front of that grenade, he didn't have to run in and do what he did. He could have stayed outside that door and *no one in this whole wide world would have reproached him or said he failed in any way to do his military duty or his human duty!* Bill didn't see it that way. He chose to save those boys, at the almost certain cost of his own life. He risked, and *gave* his life, for his belief; that an officer's first responsibility is the men beneath him. Sixteen months ago . . . I wouldn't be a father if I weren't still—brokenhearted today. . . . But I wouldn't be a soldier if I weren't *proud* today, too. I'm proud that First Army and the Chief Ordnance Officer and the Secretary of the Army have chosen to honor Bill in the way they have; I'm proud that you people are interested enough to come here and write stories and take pictures; and I'm proud most of all that Bill died *for* something and not *of* something; that he added another thread of honor to—this uniform woven of honor that we wear. (*Silence. The woman stands. Everyone stares at her.*) Helena . . . ? Helena!

RENA. Helena! (*Seeger and Rena go hastily to the woman. Seeger embraces her.*)

14

SEEGER. Where did you come from? How did you know? (*Kisses her on the cheek.*)

RENA. We didn't know where to write you, Helena. . . .

WOMAN. (*Impassively, as Rena kisses her.*) I flew in from San Francisco . . .

SEEGER. (*Still holding her hand.*) This is wonderful! We wanted you here!

RENA. San Francisco?

SEEGER. (*Turning beamingly to the others in the room.*) Gentlemen— Oh—this day gets better every minute! This is Helena, Bill's wife, my daughter-in- . . .

WOMAN. (*On "wife."*) Widow. His widow.

SEEGER. Yes, widow. Helena. My daughter-in-law! (*There are general murmurs of interest and approval. Corporal rises from his crouching position, surprised.*) How did you know about this?

HELENA. Your photograph was in the newspapers yesterday.

SEEGER. The *San Francisco* newspapers?

RENA. Why didn't you tell us that you were coming?

SEEGER. You brought the baby, didn't you? Where is he now? You'll stay with—

HELENA. (*Overlapping.*) I did not bring him. I left him with a friend.

SEEGER. Oh, no, Helena! You should have brought him!

RENA. (*A nervous laugh.*) Why have you made such a surprise of this? There are telephones . . .

SEEGER. Come. Come meet everybody. . . . (*He draws Helena u. c. McKay, Vohs, and Bonney rise. Corporal crouches again.*)

RENA. Springing up from nowhere . . .

SEEGER. Helena, this is Mr. McKay, the Assistant Secretary of the Army.

MCKAY. How do you do, Mrs. Seeger.

HELENA. How do you do. (*McKay anticipates a handshake, but Helena does not offer one.*)

MCKAY. It's a—pleasure to meet you.

HELENA. Thank you.

SEEGER. Major General Vohs . . .

VOHS. Mrs. Seeger . . .

HELENA. General.

SEEGER. Lieutenant Colonel Bonney . . .

BONNEY. How do you do, Mrs. Seeger.

15

HELENA. I remember you from Fort Colleran.

SEEGER. The Colonel was Bill's senior officer.

BONNEY. (*An uneasy smile.*) We met at the Christmas party, and at General Ramey's once or twice.

HELENA. You were Major Bonney then.

BONNEY. That's right.

HELENA. Congratulations on your promotion.

BONNEY. Thank you, Mrs. Seeger.

SEEGER. Oh, and, Helena— Come here, Dick— Helena, this is Dick Thibaudeau, my aide. Dick was with Bill at the Point!

THIBAUDEAU. How do you do, Mrs. Seeger.

HELENA. How do you do, Captain. (*Thibaudeau is holding out his hand. Helena has not offered her hand to any of the others. Now Thibaudeau waits, smiling kindly. He is 33, warm and engaging. Helena finds herself obliged to give her hand.*)

THIBAUDEAU. (*Holding Helena's hand throughout.*) I was a year ahead of Bill, and got to know him fairly well. That's why the General chose me as his aide.

SEEGER. He plays good golf; that's why I chose him!

THIBAUDEAU. Did Bill ever mention me to you?

HELENA. I don't recall—

THIBAUDEAU. I've mentioned him often, to many people. I wish he and I had served together after the Point. Knowing him is—one of my best memories.

HELENA. Thank you, Captain. You're kind.

THIBAUDEAU. Not kind; only truthful.

HELENA. Thank you. . . . (*Thibaudeau releases her hand.*)

SEEGER. Have you seen the building, Helena? The Recreation Center?

HELENA. No, I haven't.

SEEGER. Oh, wait till you do! It's the best in the whole damn Army! Bill's face would have lighted up like a Christmas tree! It's got a—

FOURTH REPORTER. General Seeger—

SEEGER. Yes? I'm sorry; I've ignored all of you. I *am* sorry.

FOURTH REPORTER. Sir, the Captain said before that you wanted no photos taken in here, but I wonder if we could have just one, of you and your wife and your daughter-in-law standing in front of the Lieutenant's portrait?

SEEGER. Yes, yes, of course! That would be a shot I'd like to have for myself! Rena, step in close here.

HELENA. (*Softly, under the above line.*) No, no . . .

SEEGER. Helena, come in a bit.

HELENA. I don't want this . . .

SEEGER. It will only take a moment. Will this be all right?

FIRST PHOTOGRAPHER. It would be better if you were all behind the desk, right up against—

HELENA. No. No pictures. No.

RENA. If she doesn't want to, Will . . .

SEEGER. (*Over Rena's line.*) Helena, it will only take a moment. We'll just do the one, and that—

HELENA. No! No pictures! (*An embarrassed silence.*)

THIBAUDEAU. Sir, I think it's time everyone . . .

SEEGER. Yes. Yes. I'm sorry, gentlemen, but— Later on we'll pose for photos. (*His momentary confusion washes away.*) Pose you clean out of flashbulbs! Captain Peck, would you take the press people down to the field?

PECK. Yes, sir.

SEEGER. Thank you all very much! I hope I'll get a chance to chat with each one of you at the luncheon! (*Helena has turned away and moves tensely L. Rena stands near, watching her with nervous concern.*) Dick, will you take Mr. McKay and General Vohs down to the platform? And Colonel Bonney?

THIBAUDEAU. Yes, sir.

PECK. (*To reporters and photographers.*) Right this way, please, ladies and gentlemen. . . .

SEEGER. (*To McKay, Vohs and Bonney, over Peck's line.*) Some of my staff officers are waiting to meet you by the reviewing platform. I hope you don't mind if I stay behind a minute or two. It's been a long time since we've seen Helena.

VOHS. Of course we don't mind.

MCKAY. She's under a good deal of strain. . . .

SEEGER. She's fine, sir. It's just—the traveling, and the excitement of all this. She's fine! Dick, we'll be down in a few minutes.

THIBAUDEAU. Yes, sir. (*Turning aside.*) Corporal, stay in the anteroom. Knock on the door in five minutes.

CORPORAL. Yes, sir.

MCKAY. I think it's a wise decision you've made, not to mention

17

the father-son relationship this afternoon. People know without our pointing to it.

SEEGER. It would have made the ceremony smaller somehow. The Army should stay impersonal, bigger than fathers and sons.

VOHS. Those things you said were quite moving, Seeger.

SEEGER. Thank you, General Vohs. Thank you. I said what I felt.

VOHS. You said it well.

THIBAUDEAU. Gentlemen . . . The elevator at the end of the hall should be waiting for us. (*Rena reaches out and tentatively touches Helena's arm. An unhurried general exodus has begun; reporters and photographers, Peck, Bonney, McKay, Vohs and Thibaudeau. Their conversations create an indistinct murmuring background. Corporal puts his clip-board on vacated swivel chair and pushes chair D. Lights in office dim to half as exodus continues. Corporal, D. L., stands behind swivel chair, leaning on the back of it.*)

CORPORAL. Generals are men built on spring-steel armatures. They move more briskly than the rest of us; come clicketing into a room willing to shake any man's hand, earnestly trying not to be proud. Their eyes have the glitter that our eyes win only after a drink or two; they're high on happiness. But their ears lean away, listening; for a twig-snap or a gun-bolt's click. Generals are men forever aware of an enemy. Generals' wives live carefully behind their teacups. They switch on sociability like a dining room chandelier, and talk of everything except pain. Their hats have flowers and their gloves are white. Generals' wives always look as though it's Mothers' Day. (*During the following, he draws the swivel chair U. into its original position below the anteroom desk.*) We corporals, watching, give nicknames to generals; Eager-Seeger, Cigar Butt; it's a way we have of pretending superiority. But we call a general the *Old Man*, too, which means that we feel a piece of our Father in him, and recognize and confirm the power in his bearing. (*Putting clip-board on desk, sitting in the chair with his back toward the imaginary wall.*) Who *is* old Seeger, we wonder. If Captain Thibaudeau hadn't told me to stay, I would have stayed anyway. And listened with both my ears. (*The lights dim on Corporal and rise to full in the office. Thibaudeau, the last to leave, is in the anteroom, about to draw closed the double doors. Helena stands R. of desk, looking up at the portrait. Seeger faces the doors.*)

18

Rena is between the two, looking from one to the other. The cyclo-rama is blue, shot with a streak of red.)

THIBAUDEAU. The Corporal from P.I.O. is out here, sir. I told him to knock in five minutes.

SEEGER. Fine, Dick, fine! Thank you! *(Thibaudeau closes double doors and exits from anteroom.)* Boy, boy, boy, boy, boy! What a day! What a day! What a day! Let me cool off for a minute! Let me grab myself a smoke! *(Unbuttoning jacket.)* Only the sun is against us!

RENA. We mustn't stay here too long. . . .

SEEGER. *(Taking off jacket.)* Oh, have I got a surprise for *you!* Have I got news! How's that for a portrait, Helena? Isn't that Bill in the breathing flesh? Had it copied from a snapshot—you know the one. Why didn't you want to pose for that photo? That would have been a great one to have; the three of us and Bill behind us. *(Going* u. *around desk.)* It's wonderful that you're here; like putting the final piece in a jigsaw puzzle! Only the baby; he ought to be here, too.

HELENA. He's a little too young to appreciate speeches.

SEEGER. *(Draping jacket on back of desk chair.)* You should have brought him, his father being honored. . . . Some day he'll ask you why he wasn't here.

RENA. *(A beat, then quickly making conversation.)* Is he with someone reliable?

HELENA. A woman I work with. She's had two of her own.

RENA. Tell us about him. Did you bring any pictures?

HELENA. *(Crosses* L. *of desk.)* No.

SEEGER. *(Taking cigar from humidor on desk.)* Now why on earth didn't you? In that one you sent from Tulsa he looked like just *any* baby; I want to see one where he looks like a Seeger! Hey, General Vohs liked what I said! Did you hear him? "Quite moving," he called it. He's a fine-looking man, isn't he? Reminds me of a judge or a— I'm *glad* now that General Del Ruth cancelled out on us! I *am!* Too big a big shot to leave his Governors Island! *(Lights cigar.)*

RENA. Helena, are you doing that accounting work again?

HELENA. It's economic research. Yes, I am.

RENA. I forget. . . . Have you found a nice place to live?

SEEGER. Listen, I'm holding in a piece of news and I'm going to burst if I don't sing it out! McKay, the Assistant Secretary—and that cold way of his, that's part of being a good executive; underneath he's warm and friendly—well, driving over here from the Guest House, he told me as plain as could be that when the next promotion list comes out—this second star of mine will be made permanent!

RENA. Oh, Will! Oh, thank God!

SEEGER. Major General. *Permanent!* That's five more years for certain! I'll be sixty-two before they boot me out!

RENA. (*Going to him, embracing, kissing him.*) Oh, Will, I'm so happy for you, darling! For both of us! I knew it would happen! I knew! He's been so worried about being retired! I told you not to worry!

SEEGER. (*Holding Rena in his arms.*) "It's a wonderful day," I said, and he said, "I think you'll be having another wonderful day when the new list is published!" Isn't that telling me plain?

RENA. I knew they wouldn't let go of you!

SEEGER. Five more years! You bet I was worried! Five more years!

HELENA. (*Crossing D.*) Congratulations, Major General. Permanent. (*Her sardonic tone hangs in the air. Rena kisses Seeger's cheek, as though to distract him.*)

RENA. Oh, Will! Will . . .

SEEGER. What's wrong, Helena? Are you angry? Because you weren't invited here? How could we invite you when we didn't know where you were? It's you who put this—hole between us.

RENA. She's here now; there's no point in discussing it. . . .

SEEGER. (*Freeing himself of Rena.*) No, no, we have to discuss it sooner or later.

HELENA. I'm not angry because I wasn't invited.

SEEGER. Why did you just—vanish from Tulsa that way? We wrote you, wrote to people at the Fort. . . .

HELENA. You didn't think I would spend the rest of my life at Colleran, did you? I stayed there to have Billy, and then I left.

SEEGER. Why San Francisco? Why not here or New York; that was your home.

HELENA. I chose to go west.

SEEGER. But why didn't you let us know where you were? Rena has been making excuses for you all year, but now—I don't believe them. . . . Why didn't you write? (*Helena turns away.*) You and Billy are our family, Helena, and we're yours. To cut us apart this way . . . (*Rena steps D.*)

20

HELENA. Bill was the only connection between us.

RENA. (*Turning* R.) We should go . . .

SEEGER. (*To Rena.*) Plenty of time. (*To Helena.*) Then don't we owe it to Bill to *keep* the connection, now that he's gone? Rena and I never got to know you as well as we wanted, but that was because of my duty in Europe. It was going to be different when I got here; you know that. I was going to have Bill reassigned; you would have been in one of those houses right up on the Circle. . . .

RENA. Tell me, please, where is the sense in bringing up the past and what-would-have-been?

SEEGER. Rena, will you stop interrupting every time I open my mouth? You are as nervous today as—

HELENA. (*Cutting in on "nervous."*) Oh, yes, General, you were going to have Bill reassigned! (*A beat. There is a challenge in her tone that disquiets Seeger.*)

RENA. Will . . .

SEEGER. You're right; the past is—past! You're here now, Helena, and that's what counts. This day has brought us together again and we're going to stay together! We're going to write to each other and visit, see that little Billy-Boy—I *wish* you'd brought a picture of him! Do you know why Rena is so on edge? Because this is the first time she has been out of the house before five P.M. in more than a month! This woman is a television fan! She has sold her soul to that seventeen-inch screen! Sits in the living room all day in an old green bathrobe with the blinds pulled down; pretty soon they're going to give her one of those Academy Awards for just watching! It's Saturday, Rena! Relax! You're not missing any of your quiz shows or dancing teen-agers!

RENA. Please . . .

SEEGER. I'm teasing, Rena, I'm teasing!

HELENA. Whose idea was this ceremony today?

SEEGER. Idea? Why, it was no one's idea! It's a tradition; an important building is dedicated to a hero; that's Army tradition.

HELENA. Who chose Bill for the dedication?

SEEGER. (*A beat.*) McKay, General Del Ruth. The Chief Ordnance Officer, the Secretary. The same men who decided to build the building in the first place. Decisions like that come from higher up, 'way high up.

HELENA. *How* did those men choose Bill?

SEEGER. Well . . . a list of names was submitted to them. Possible candidates. . . . This is an Ordnance post; they wanted someone in Ordnance. The building is for enlisted men; they wanted either an enlisted man or an officer who had performed some outstanding deed for enlisted men.

HELENA. Who put Bill's name on the list?

SEEGER. Well, I did. There's nothing against regulations in that. Because I'm in command doesn't mean my son should be disqualified from an honor.

RENA. Will didn't try to influence them; *they* made the decision. . . .

SEEGER. Right, and you can bet your life they bent over backwards to be impartial! Army honors are weighed out as carefully as gold! They chose Bill on his merits, not as any favor to me.

HELENA. I am wasting my talents plotting population curves. I ought to be a mystic. I can pick up a newspaper, read a paragraph, look at a smiling picture, and say, "This is all happening because he *planned* it to happen! A celebration day for General Seeger!"

SEEGER. For me? For Bill, Helena! My God, you sound as though you don't *want* him to be honored! Wait till you see that building! A million and a half dollars of the best facilities an army ever gave its men! There's a swimming pool that's the biggest in the whole state! There are handball courts and a basketball court that Bill would have given his eyeteeth to play on! There's a library with—

HELENA. (*Cutting in on "play on."*) Bill was not an athlete! He did not take after you in that respect.

SEEGER. Oh, no, Helena, you're wrong there. Remember, Rena, when we were at Chaffee, the basketball? No, no, it was Fort Leavenworth, Command School— (*To Helena.*) Fort Leavenworth. There was a basketball hoop on the side of our garage, and Bill was out there every evening before dinner for a solid hour, practicing foul-shots. No stopping him. (*To Rena.*) How old was he? Twelve? Thirteen?

HELENA. There were tournaments for the officers' children. He practiced because if he played badly you would be short with him for a week or two. You remember what you want to remember; you forget what you want to forget.

RENA. Will . . .

SEEGER. What do you mean? I was never short with him. He *liked* basketball. He liked handball, too, and tennis. He was a *fine* athlete. We played handball every Saturday afternoon for two—

HELENA. (*Cutting in on "every."*) He liked those sports because he was afraid not to like them, for fear *you* wouldn't like *him.*

SEEGER. That's crazy! You think I don't know what Bill liked? Just show me another father and son—

HELENA. (*Overlapping, starting on "liked."*) That's exactly what I think! Did you ever *ask* what he liked? All that counted was what *you* liked, what *you* wanted, what *you*—

SEEGER. (*Overlapping, starting on "all."*) What? I didn't have to ask; I *knew* what he liked! He and I were—

RENA. (*Cutting both of them off.*) Stop it! He's dead! Stop! He's dead. . . . What difference does it make what he liked or didn't like? He's dead. Stop talking about him. . . . (*A pause.*)

HELENA. There speaks the mother. What kind of mother are you, Rena? This is your *son* we're talking about, *not some dead horse lying in the gutter!*

SEEGER. Shut up that kind of talk.

HELENA. (*Turning to Seeger.*) Don't you give orders to me, General! I haven't joined the Army! Major General . . . Permanent . . . Do you know what part of your speech I loved best? Do you know what part made me *most proud* to be a member of your family? "When the son dies, the father dies, too." Oh, there is a line! There is a noble line! (*Seeger turns* R.) *What son? What father?* You're not dead! Bill is under the grass at Arlington, what was left of him, but you're here, standing, with your shoulders full of stars and your head full of speeches, smoking cigars and posing for photographs! *Who* died when Bill died? She? Oh, no, *she* died when she was born! *I* died when Bill died! *I* died! (*Pointing at her eyes.*) Have I slept one night in sixteen months? (*A pause.*)

SEEGER. (*Turning to Helena.*) Why have you come here? This is a day for—pride and happiness, and you've brought hatred.

HELENA. For you; for him, love. I've come here to stop this.

SEEGER. To stop what?

HELENA. This whole day; your parade, your luncheon, your dedication.

SEEGER. Am I—awake?

RENA. Leave her, Will.

HELENA. A memorial of this kind will spin Bill in his grave like a stick in a whirlpool. He detested you and he despised your Army. For thirty-one years you held his arms in your bully's grip and

23

pushed him where you pleased. He's dead now; today you let go. (*A pause.*)

RENA. Listen to me, Will. She's speaking from spite. She didn't know Bill as well as—

SEEGER. (*Interrupting on "didn't," not turning from Helena.*) Be quiet, Rena.

RENA. No, I won't be quiet. A mother knows her son better than his wife ever—

SEEGER. (*Turning now, on "wife."*) Quiet, damn it! (*Turns to Helena again.*)

RENA. (*Softly.*) Oh, dear God . . . (*She sinks into chair,* U. R.)

SEEGER. I pushed him, did I?

HELENA. From the day he was born; into games, into races, into the Point, into a career that was a prison cell. You had a simple trick of turning your back on him. He could never say "no" to it. You robbed him young of that word.

SEEGER. (*Crossing to* L. *of Helena.*) You make me sick, every one of your generation. "Hands off"—that should be the policy, eh? Mustn't tamper with the tender children; "father" is a dirty word! What was the awful sin of *your* father, a little drinking now and then?

HELENA. Backwards, General; a little sobriety now and then. Let's leave *my* happy childhood out of this.

SEEGER. (*Loses temper.*) Well, try childhood the way I had it. Try it with *no* father and *no* mother, in a God-damned orphanage where nobody even cares enough to give you a *slap* once in a while, let alone a kiss! Try it that way and maybe you'll change your mind a little! What do you think a father's for? To sit back and ignore a boy? Let him feel his own way, as though nobody'd ever lived and learned before him? Maybe I was wrong to buy Bill a bicycle! Maybe I should have let him invent the wheel himself! (*Crosses* R., *paces.*) Sure, I pushed him! You bet I did! I pushed him where he belonged, and he was happy! Games and races? We celebrated more times than we hung up crepe, I can tell you that! The Point? We celebrated there, too; eighteenth man in a class of four hundred and nine!

HELENA. And he belonged there and was happy? Oh, ho, ho! Get a ouija board and ask Bill's ghost about West Point! They spotted him for The Outsider the minute he stepped through those gates. Ask him about the jolly cadets with the picturesque nicknames;

24

Froggy and Boots and Candy-Bar. Ask him about the jolly hazings dished out to The Outsider, because Froggy and Boots and so on were *Insiders, Army!* Sadists, they were. . . .

SEEGER. Oh, don't give me that crap about the hazings! Dick Thibaudeau got the same treatment and laughs about it! Every man who's been to the—

HELENA. (*Cutting in on "who's."*) Dick Thibaudeau was there because he wanted to be there!

SEEGER. (*Crossing* D. *to Helena.*) And so was Bill! Not at first maybe, I'll grant you that, but after a while. . . . It's the only foundation for an Army career! These would be three stars, not two, if I'd been at the Point! Bill knew how important it was.

HELENA. Maybe you didn't hear me before. Bill despised the Army. He didn't *want* an Army career.

SEEGER. (*Crosses* R. *to chair, sits.*) You're out of your mind. I know what he wanted. He was my son. . . .

HELENA. You never knew what he wanted, nor did you care! He was a link to you—you said it yourself in that lovely speech of yours—a link in a chain, to be shaped and hammered and pounded, not a person to be cared for, to be loved. Did you ever try to see a quarter of an inch behind that strapped-on smile of his? Don't tell me you did, General, because I'll call you a liar to your face!

RENA. (*Rises, crosses* D. *to* L. *of Helena.*) How dare you! How dare you speak to this man this way! You think you have all—

SEEGER. (*Cutting in on "think."*) All right, Rena . . .

RENA. No! You let me speak now, Will! You let me speak! You think you have all the truth laid out in front of you; well you haven't, Helena. I know things that— We were on the ship coming back from Europe when Bill—when the awful cable—they handed it to us. . . . You think Will didn't care. . . . He cried, Helena.

SEEGER. (*Rises, crosses to window* R.) Oh, Rena . . .

RENA. *He cried!* With his face in my lap, he cried so hard that soon I wasn't crying for Bill any more but for *him,* because I thought his heart was going to break in two!

SEEGER. Oh, for . . .

RENA. And there's more truth than *that* you don't know about; times when Bill was sick and he took *leave time* to stay home and sit with him! Years when we were scraping along on captain's pay and he spent half of it on toys he'd promised Bill! So don't you

25

ever dare say again that he didn't love him! You don't know *every-thing!* You *think* you do, but you don't! (*A pause.*)

SEEGER. That's from watching television. (*Rena stands motionless, her eyes closed tight.*)

RENA. Will, oh, Will, there are moments when I hate you so much! (*A pause.*)

HELENA. Were you crying for Bill or for yourself?

SEEGER. (*Crossing* u. *behind desk.*) Are you coming to the parade, Helena?

HELENA. Listen to me, General! Don't be fooled by that soft "A" on the end of my name. I tacked that on for style after I won the Battle of the Bronx. I'm Helen Riker; I'm a gutter-fighter from 'way back, and I tell you now to stop these ceremonies. Don't force me to use all my ammunition, because I'll blow this room sky-high. Bill wanted no dedication. Stop these ceremonies. (*SOUND: A marching band sneaks in very softly in the distance, bugles, field drums, bass drum and cymbals.*)

RENA. What kind of threats are you making? What do you mean, ammunition?

SEEGER. (*Taking up jacket.*) She doesn't mean anything.

HELENA. He didn't want his name on Army buildings! (*Thibaudeau comes briskly into the anteroom, followed by a Private in parade uniform.*)

SEEGER. (*Thrusting his arms into his jacket.*) She's talking, that's all. We've listened to her long enough. Just talk. If you don't want to see your husband being paid one of the highest tributes the Army can pay a man, then you can just stay—	THIBAUDEAU. I told you to knock, Corporal. CORPORAL. (*Rising.*) I was just about to, sir. (*Resumes seat.*) THIBAUDEAU. (*Rapping on double door.*) Sir! It's Thibaudeau.

HELENA. I'm not bluffing, General! I did not fly here because I like flying. (*Seeger looks at her uncertainly for a moment, his jacket still unbuttoned. Thibaudeau raps again.*)

THIBAUDEAU. Sir?

SEEGER. Come in, Dick! (*Thibaudeau enters; Private follows.*)

THIBAUDEAU. The Corporal should have knocked, sir. The troops have left the six hundred area. They'll be here in a few minutes. (*He signals Private to General's flag,* R. *of desk. During following, Private takes flag from stand and exits* L. *with it.*)

26

SEEGER. Right, right . . .

THIBAUDEAU. McKay, Vohs and Bonney are already on the platform.

SEEGER. (*Rubbing his hands indecisively.*) Plenty of time . . .

THIBAUDEAU. I arranged a place on the platform for Mrs. Seeger. (*Indicating Helena.*)

SEEGER. She won't be there. She isn't feeling well.

THIBAUDEAU. Oh—I'm sorry. I carry a small infirmary of aspirins and sedatives. . . .

HELENA. No, thank you, Captain. (*Sits coldly in a chair* D. R. *of desk.*)

SEEGER. Dick, will you take my wife downstairs?

THIBAUDEAU. Yes, sir.

RENA. Aren't you—?

SEEGER. I want to speak to Helena for a minute. Go along with Dick.

RENA. I want to stay here.

SEEGER. Go with Dick, Rena. I want to speak to her alone.

THIBAUDEAU. There's really not much time, sir.

SEEGER. I'll be down. Don't worry.

RENA. Will, I don't want you to—

SEEGER. (*Cutting her off on "want."*) Do as I tell you, Rena!

RENA. (*Pause.*) Handbag . . . (*Goes* U. *to desk.*)

SEEGER. (*To Thibaudeau.*) I'll join you on the platform. Don't worry. (*Lights dim to half in office and come up full on Corporal. During the following, Rena takes handbag from desk and exits with Thibaudeau. Seeger closes double doors and remains facing them.*)

CORPORAL. Do you hear the band? It's half a mile away, marching toward us through the gray, deserted barracks of the post. Bugles, field drums, a bass drum and cymbals. Nine companies march behind and thirteen more wait along the way, marking time, ready to affix themselves to the parade's growing body. Twenty-two companies in all; two hundred men in each; four thousand four hundred men marching ten abreast; boots, cartridge belts, helmets, rifles. Closer they will come, watched by KP's on a smoke-break, and by a furious dog from somewhere, and by the children of the post; quiet children, already tutored in respect. Some of these will put a midgets' tail to the parade, their feet in sneakers keeping careful time with the feet in boots. Straight toward the side of this

27

building the parade will march, and then column left by companies onto the field below. The shoulders of the men will be numb under the weight of their rifles; their helmets will be ovens, the sweatbands dripping, teasing their faces. "Eyes right!" Two hundred heads will snap right, and two hundred more, and two hundred more, and two hundred more—and each of the four thousand four hundred men will see for an eye-flick, on the reviewing stand, General Seeger, perspiring no less than they, his arm locked in perpetual salute, motionless as an arm of steel or stone, as the arm of a statue; "Man Saluting." (*Lights dim on Corporal and come up full in the office. The red streak on the cyclorama, having swollen imperceptibly throughout the preceding scene, is now a wide gash across the blueness, still swelling. Seeger turns from the double doors to face Helena, seated* R. C. *During this scene the sound of the distant band grows slowly, steadily louder.*)

SEEGER. You think you understood Bill, but you didn't, and you don't understand me, either. Marrying you was—wrong for him. I don't mean that as criticism of *you*, Helena; you're an admirable woman and I'm fond of you, whether or not you believe I am. But it's wrong for Army to marry away from Army. Rena, now; her father was a battalion commander on the post where I made first lieutenant. She understands things about me and about Bill that you'll never understand; things we feel. . . .

HELENA. "Army." You make it sound like a religion.

SEEGER. I do; I guess I do. You know the joke line, "He found a home in the Army"? That's *me*, Helena. . . . You don't know what it's like to begin your life in a foundling home. No roots, nobody behind you; not even a real name, but one some social worker *made up* for you. . . . Who are you? Where do you come from? Where are you going? You're more alone than—anyone on earth. Make your own bed when you're six years old. You haven't even got God, because it's a no-denomination service and they're going to let you *choose* your god when you're old enough! How can you really believe when it's up to you to choose! (*Crosses* U. *of desk.*) The day I was eighteen I ran away and joined up. The Army assigned me a serial number, Helena, that was *me* and nobody else! They put—a *path* in front of me; "Go up through those ranks!" They gave me fathers, my officers, and they gave me gods, too, the highest brass, the McKays and the General Del Ruths. *System* they gave me!—you get an order, you obey the order; you get the

28

first stripe, the second . . . When you come into a new post, you check the bulletin board and you know where you stand! (*Buttons a few buttons of his jacket.*) I *had* to pass it on to Bill! You find something good, you pass it on; that's what parents are for! I'm a Christian. I raised him Christian; you don't call me a bully for that, do you? I'm American; I raised him American; is that being a bully? You know what he wanted to do? Did he tell you *that*? Seventeen years old he comes to me, he wants to finish high school and go away to the oil fields in Texas, work in the oil fields! "Are you afraid you won't do well at the Point?" "No, Papa, I just want to work in the oil fields." Was I supposed to say yes to that? Some book he'd read about drilling for oil . . . When he came to his senses he would have been too old for the Point, and without the Point he would have got no higher than I am now; commanding the class B training camps, or pushing supplies up for the generals with *four* stars and their faces on the front pages! I wanted him to go higher than me! That's progress! That's human! I know I did something risky. I'm not as dumb as you think I am. If a man hasn't got some soldier in him, you can't force him to *be* a soldier, and it's wrong trying. I know that. *Plenty* of nights I laid awake, wondering if I was hurting Bill more than I was helping him. . . . Now I'm going to tell you something, Helena. Yes, I cried on that ship when I got the news—not as much as Rena said, but I cried, and for Bill, not for me—but *after* I cried, Helena, afterwards . . . I stretched out, and I went to sleep! And I slept well that night, and I've slept well ever since. Because the way Bill died told me I'd been *right*. Suppose he *was* unhappy for a week or two at the Point! Suppose he *did* have a few days when he thought he'd like to be an oil man, or a doctor, or a—barber or a plumber! The end is what counts! And the end is that he was a *soldier*, or he would have let those men die without risking his own skin to save them! And if he was that much of a soldier at the end, then there was some soldier in him at the beginning, too, and I was *right* in everything I did with him! You said before he detested me. I don't think he did, but if he did, then maybe that's the price of being a good father. The mother is soft, and she gets the love; the father is hard, and he gets hatred. But it's the father who makes the son a man. Well, I made Bill more than a man; I made him a soldier, a gallant soldier! That's not me talking now, that's a bronze plaque on a million-and-a-half dollar building! "First Lieutenant William J.

Seeger, Junior; a gallant soldier and an exemplary officer." Those words have come down from the very top of the Army; and they speak louder and clearer and will last a thousand years longer than anything you've said this morning! (*Completing buttoning of his jacket.*)

HELENA. Blind . . . Blind . . . Blind man. . . . You see what you want to see; you hear what you want to hear. . . . (*Rising.*) Blind man, your plaque is mistaken! (*Seeger takes cap from desk, starts for door.*) He *wasn't* a gallant soldier! He was sick and despairing, miserable at Colleran and at every post before Colleran! (*Seeger stops, turns to face Helena angrily.*) He *wasn't* an exemplary officer! He kept a bottle in his desk and another under the edge of the mattress! Drinks pinned him together and kept him walking; drinks, and you pushing him!

SEEGER. (*Going toward her as if to strike her.*) Liar! You filthy God-damned liar! I'll slam that—

HELENA. He didn't give his life to save enlisted men! (*Seeger's upraised arm freezes.*) He gave his life because he could no longer bear to keep it! Because you and your Army had grabbed onto it so tight that giving it was his only way to get free!

SEEGER. What are you saying?

HELENA. (*Stepping towards him.*) Suicide! He committed suicide! How big do I have to paint it to pull open your eyes? He committed suicide! You blind man . . . (*SOUND: The band, no more than a block away now, yields to the field drums. They rip out a hard, rasping beat, repetitive, increasingly loud. The cyclorama is now almost entirely red.*) Fathers and gods, those men who stood here? He saw them clear, and he *envied* your blindness! A path you gave him? Broken glass to nowhere! He chose the short cut.

SEEGER. (*Turning to door.*) It couldn't be. . . .

HELENA. (*Near tears.*) It was! It was! And still you won't let go! Still you're bullying him!

SEEGER. There were—witnesses. . . . A roomful. . . .

HELENA. *I* am the witness! *I saw his heart!*

SEEGER. (*Turning towards her.*) You're— You— There was— *whiskey* on your breath when I kissed you before! There's whiskey in what you're saying now! You're—a bitter, vengeful woman, who's made—a career of her widowhood! (*Crossing L. to door.*)

30

Corporal! (*Corporal rises.*) Is he still there? (*Pulls open one wing of double doors.*) Corporal!

CORPORAL. Yes, sir!

SEEGER. Come in here! Bitter, vengeful . . . (*Corporal enters office.*)

HELENA. No, no. . . . It's for *his* sake . . . !

SEEGER. (*Has taken a key ring from his pocket and is detaching a key. To Corporal.*) I'm giving you a key. Key to this door. You lock it behind me and you don't unlock it until I come back. She doesn't get out; nobody else gets in. You understand that? (*Gives key to Corporal.*)

CORPORAL. Yes, sir.

SEEGER. You lock it behind me. And she doesn't go near that window.

CORPORAL. Yes, sir. (*A beat. Seeger, meeting Helena's gaze, puts on his cap.*)

HELENA. All right, General, you *have* your parade! Stand in the sun and salute your Army! Three cheers for gods, and systems, and straight paths, and uniforms woven of honor! But I swear to you—I swear by his body in that box at Arlington—you'll dedicate no building this afternoon. I swear that. (*SOUND: The drums stop. A respite of silence.*)

SEEGER. You don't believe in *anything,* that's your trouble. And you want everyone else to be as poisoned as you are. Bill was a fine soldier in a fine army. He was proud and he was happy.

HELENA. Go to your parade, blind man! (*SOUND: An explosion of brass and percussion. The band is directly below the window, blasting out a strident, deafening march. Seeger wheels and quickly exits. Corporal closes the double doors, locks them. Cyclorama is entirely red, with sun-glints from the brass instruments chasing across it. Corporal turns to face Helena. She stands R. C., her hands clapped over her ears against the din. SOUND: Under the crashing of the band, the thud of marching feet.*)

VOICE. (*Shouting below.*) Column left . . . HAR! (*Helena is crying now, no longer able to sustain her armor of hardness. Corporal moves a step toward her, tucking the key into his breast pocket. Helena's body shakes with sobs. She collapses into the chair R. C. There is only the sight of her crying; the sound of it is buried under the bugles and the drums and the cymbals. Corporal is drawn slowly toward her.*)

ANOTHER VOICE. Column left . . . HAR! (*Corporal stands near Helena, watching her with compassion. He reaches out and touches her shoulder in an ineffectual soothing gesture. He looks at the audience. THE CURTAIN FALLS.*)

END OF ACT I

ACT II

AT RISE: *The band can still be heard, stationed now at the far end of the parade field. The cyclorama is a blanched noon-day blue. Helena is seated as before, no longer crying, a handkerchief balled in her hands. Corporal lounges against Seeger's desk, smoking a cigarette, watching Helena. He crosses to the window, peers out through the slats of the blind.*

CORPORAL. Oop, there goes number six. (*A downward swing of his forearm, accompanied by a sibilant sound-effect.*) Sssssssss-eeeeeeep— Pww!

HELENA. How many men have to pass out before they end the parade?

CORPORAL. Well, there are two ambulances that haven't even opened their doors yet. (*Turning from the window.*) Don't worry; of the six men who have dropped so far, maybe one was genuine. The other five are just getting excused from future parades. (*Helena is silent. Corporal returns to* C.) Why don't you take a little drink, Mrs. Seeger. . . . (*Helena shakes her head.*) He's finished inspecting them; they're moving out now. (*Helena smooths the handkerchief and holds it out. Corporal takes it, holds it for a moment, then puts it in his pocket.*) Would you like to talk about your husband? I would like to listen.

HELENA. You heard from out there?

CORPORAL. Almost everything. (*A pause. Corporal sits against the edge of the desk, crushing out his cigarette in ashtray. Helena looks at her hands. SOUND: The music of the band diminishes and grows distant during the following speech.*)

HELENA. My husband . . . was a man who . . . held himself in contempt. The Army sickened him, but he sickened himself more, because he couldn't leave the Army any more than a tree can leave the ground. His father had rooted him too deeply; in the uniform, the tradition, the manliness, the honor. . . . He hated

33

himself for not ripping away the uniform, but secretly and more sharply, I think he hated himself . . . for not *loving* the uniform. . . . But, oh, the face of him! That ringmaster smile! Two drinks at a party and he could tell a joke in a way that would make a statue laugh; twinkle an eye so that every woman in the room went soft and boneless. Three drinks and he fell silent. Four, and I would edge toward our coats, because with five and six he sometimes began to—shiver, like a child in the dark. . . . Did you offer me a cigarette before? (*Corporal rises, taking a pack of cigarettes from his pocket.*) He picked me up in Rockefeller Plaza. He was on leave. My handbag spilled and he chased my rolling compact, in the best tradition of romantic movies. (*Corporal offers her a cigarette.*) Thank you. (*Corporal strikes a match, holds it for her.*) Five years ago. His uniform fooled me. That's the double feature. (*Corporal sits on a nearby chair.*) I thought I had finally found someone stronger than I had had to be. It was a short honeymoon, though. Loving him was pushing a log uphill. His reasoning was simple; he was contemptible, therefore I, who said I loved him, was either a liar or a fool. I said it loud! With my heart! He turned to—other women, who made no claim of loving. Or who proved to him, perhaps, beyond a doubt, how truly contemptible he was. . . . Well, I am not a saint. Compassion and understanding I had, but selfishness came stronger. Toward the end I found myself . . . beginning to share his contempt. No more I-love-you's. I think I might have left him, if not for the baby on its way. . . . I owe him this one deed today; to put the knife in that father of his.

CORPORAL. Do you believe that somewhere . . . he's watching you? (*A pause.*)

HELENA. I owe him this. (*A pause, and then an imperative knock at the door, L.*)

SEEGER. Corporal. (*Corporal rises, looking at Helena, then goes to door, taking key from pocket. Helena rises. Seeger knocks again.*) Corporal. It's General Seeger. (*Corporal looks back at Helena.*)

HELENA. Unlock it. (*Corporal unlocks the door and opens it. Seeger enters, removing his cap. His face is running with perspiration. His eyes go to Helena firmly and with authority. SOUND: The band is now far away, but still faintly audible.*)

CORPORAL. Sir. (*Seeger turns. Corporal gives him the key.*)

SEEGER. Thank you. (*A beat. Corporal exits L. into anteroom, stands facing office. Seeger puts cap on desk and wipes face with handkerchief, his eyes on Helena again. She meets them unflinch-ingly.)*

HELENA. What was the final score? How many men passed out? *(Seeger does not answer. He has regained the certainty which he lost before leaving for the parade. Thibaudeau, cap in hand, enters anteroom and continues into office, followed by Private carrying Seeger's flag. Thibaudeau stands waiting L. C. Private places flag in stand L. of desk.)*

THIBAUDEAU. I hope you're feeling better, Mrs. Seeger.

HELENA. *(Extinguishing cigarette.)* I am. *(Private steps back, salutes flag.)*

THIBAUDEAU. You missed a very smart parade. Very smart. *(Private exits L.)* Or did you watch from the window?

SEEGER. Close the door, please. *(Thibaudeau closes the door, L. Corporal sits in swivel chair, facing office. Seeger, unbuttoning jacket moves U. R.)*

HELENA. What's happening here?

SEEGER. Sit down, Dick. *(Thibaudeau takes a seat L. C. Seeger, by the air-conditioning unit, flaps the sides of his jacket against his sweat-stained shirt.)*

HELENA. What is this?

SEEGER. Dick, I'd like you to tell my daughter-in-law what you told me. On the platform.

THIBAUDEAU. Yes, sir. Well, the General asked me if I thought that Bill—Lieutenant Seeger—if I thought that he was ever un-happy at the Point, and I said, quite the contrary; he was one of the most—*contented* men there. He was extremely popular, both with his classmates and with the men in the classes above him, and though he did his full job of studying, he still found time to par-ticipate in just about every activity available. And not only par-ticipate, but help organize. He had a great natural flair for lead-ership.

SEEGER. And those bull-sessions . . .

THIBAUDEAU. Yes. He and I had a number of bull-sessions where he said more than once that he could have kicked himself for not wanting to come to the Point originally. We mapped out the careers that we hoped were ahead of us, and Bill thanked his lucky stars that the General had put some sense into his head. *(Helena watches Thibaudeau blankly. Seeger is looking from one*

35

to the other, doing his best not to show his satisfaction and relief.
SOUND: The band is gone now. Complete silence.)

SEEGER. I suppose he was a *bit* unhappy at the beginning. . . .

THIBAUDEAU. Of course he was. Good Lord, everyone is. Except maybe the men who've been to a military prep school. You come into this whole new world of discipline and regulations . . . It takes two or three weeks until you're oriented. After that, though —well, there just isn't any better education *anywhere*, military or non-military. That's *my* belief, and it was Bill's, too. (*A pause. Seeger moves towards desk. Thibaudeau sits forward, ready to rise.*)

SEEGER. Thank you very much, Dick. You go along to the Club now, and I'll be over in a few minutes. Tell Mr.—

HELENA. (*On "minutes."*) Were you a close friend of my husband, Captain?

THIBAUDEAU. Yes, I was. As I told you before, knowing him is one of my best memories.

HELENA. If you and he were such close friends, how do you account for the fact that he never mentioned you to me?

THIBAUDEAU. Perhaps you forgot.

HELENA. I'm not a forgetter.

THIBAUDEAU. I wasn't his *closest* friend, Mrs. Seeger. That was a fellow named Holly, or Holliday.

HELENA. Holland.

THIBAUDEAU. Holland; yes, that's right. (*Sitting back in chair.*) But I was a *close* friend of Bill's nonetheless. If he never mentioned me, well then, I'm probably not as memorable a person as he was. (*Seeger smiles, takes a cigar from humidor.*)

HELENA. You said before that you were a year ahead of Bill at the Point.

THIBAUDEAU. That's right.

HELENA. But still you accepted him as a close friend?

THIBAUDEAU. He was popular beyond his own class, as I also said. There was this flair for leadership. He had a—an aura of— *belonging*. It was *he* who accepted *me*. (*A pause. Seeger lights his cigar.*)

HELENA. Captain, wasn't my husband subjected to unusual hazing at the Point?

THIBAUDEAU. Hazing is part of the Point, Mrs. Seeger. Outsiders exaggerate its significance by about three thousand per cent.

36

HELENA. I said *unusual* hazing.

THIBAUDEAU. No, he wasn't subjected to unusual hazing.

SEEGER. I didn't think you were going to be cross-examined. I'm sorry.

HELENA. Bill told me that during his first few months at the Point he expressed criticism of its procedures and of military training in general, and as a result of this he was subjected to *barbaric hazing* until the day he became an upperclassman!

SEEGER. (*On "until."*) Barbaric!

THIBAUDEAU. That is not true. It just isn't true, Mrs. Seeger.

HELENA. Then why did he lie to me, perhaps you can tell me that. Because either he lied or you are lying now. (*Crosses* D. L. *a beat.*)

SEEGER. Or you're lying, Helena.

THIBAUDEAU. (*Helena crosses* D. R.) Sir, I don't think anybody's lying. Mrs. Seeger, I told *my* wife about some of the hazings *I* received, and I frankly confess I made them sound a heck of a lot worse than they were, just as I've exaggerated some of my combat experiences to her; because when I do, she goes all big-eyed, and starts clucking over me, and it makes me feel like—Paul Bunyan or somebody! I think maybe that's what Bill did with you.

HELENA. The hazings that Bill described did not make him a hero to me. *Shall I list some of the obscenities?*

SEEGER. (*Crosses* D. R. *of desk.*) Now, damn it, that's enough! Those hazings are regulated!

THIBAUDEAU. That's the truth, Mrs. Seeger.

SEEGER. That's the U. S. Military Academy, part of the Army, not a—trade school full of leather-jacket hoodlums!

HELENA. How would *you* know, you with your visitor's pass! (*A pause.*)

SEEGER. I wasn't lucky enough to attend the Point, but I know that when you speak of obscenities and barbaric hazings, you are wrong. Dead wrong. I know that. (*Crosses* U. *of desk, looks out window,* C. *A beat.*)

HELENA. Froggy, and Boots, and Candy-Bar. Did you know those men? (*A beat.*)

THIBAUDEAU. Yes, I did.

HELENA. Am I dead wrong?

THIBAUDEAU. They never went after Bill, Mrs. Seeger.

SEEGER. (*Crosses* D. R. *of desk.*) Who? What men?

HELENA. Leather-jacket hoodlums!

SEEGER. What . . . ?

THIBAUDEAU. Sir, the Point gets a cross-section of men, just as any school does. I don't necessarily mean a social cross-section, but a psychological one. They do a more careful job than other schools of sifting out the undesirables, but still, now and then one is bound to slip through.

SEEGER. Well, of course, yes, there's bound to be a bad apple somewhere in the basket. Of course . . .

THIBAUDEAU. When Bill and I were there, there *was* this *very small group* of men who were—pretty disturbed emotionally, and the custom of hazing *did* provide them with—an easy outlet for their disturbances. They made some of the plebes do things that went far beyond the usual bracings and push-ups, and I guess there's no doubt that they were a group of—sick men. Bill was never one of their targets, though; they went after the fellows who were—well, misfits in one way or another. I suppose they justified themselves as—"guardians of the Army's purity."

HELENA. They went after Bill.

THIBAUDEAU. No, ma'am, they did not.

SEEGER. Nobody reported these men?

THIBAUDEAU. Well, sir, you know . . . At that age, reporting someone, it—it hardly seems at all like being a soldier. The authorities found them out, though; don't you worry about that. Not a one of them is in the Army today. The ringleader, the one called Candy-Bar, he was expelled from the Point in his final year.

HELENA. They went after Bill.

SEEGER. Are you—sure that they didn't? When I think there's even a *chance* that . . .

THIBAUDEAU. Yes, sir, I am sure. It was very well known just which men they were badgering. Half a dozen—misfits, as I said. Complainers, fellows who rode the sick-book . . .

HELENA. Do you think I pulled those names out of the air? Bill told me about them! Froggy and Boots and—

THIBAUDEAU. (*On "Boots."*) And he said they badgered *him?*

HELENA. *Tormented* him! Endlessly! (*To Seeger.*) I am not lying! (*A pause. Seeger looks anxiously towards Thibaudeau.*)

THIBAUDEAU. (*Seeger crosses* u. *of desk.*) Mrs. Seeger, I'm going to say something presumptuous, and I hope you won't take offense at it. I'm interested in psychology. I read every book I can

38

on the subject, and though I'm not an authority, I'm not a dabbler, either. It seems to me that when a person, a woman particularly, suffers the kind of loss that you've suffered, she's apt to look around and choose a scapegoat to strike out at. I think you've chosen the Point. I guess you feel that if Bill hadn't gone into the Army he'd still be alive, and so you're saying that he was unhappy at the Point, that he was against military procedure, that he was singled out for unusual hazing. . . . It's not true, Mrs. Seeger. Obviously Bill told you about Candy-Bar and the others, but I can't believe he told you they bothered *him*, because what reason would he have had for lying to you?

HELENA. I am imagining things, then . . .

THIBAUDEAU. No, I think what you're doing is simply—deflecting some of the grief of Bill's death. But you seem to me a strong enough woman to accept reality without the—well, it's a neurotic shield you're carrying around—forgive me, please—and the sooner you put it down, the sooner the grief will go away. Everything I said about Bill at the Point was true. He was the last man those fellows would have gone after. He *belonged*. (*A pause. Helena turns away.*)

SEEGER. Thank you. Thank you, Dick, very much.

THIBAUDEAU. (*Rises.*) I'd better get over to the Club and make sure McKay and Vohs are getting the good liquor.

SEEGER. (*Smiling.*) And cover for me; tell them I'll be there in five minutes.

HELENA. (*Quietly, still facing away.*) How did you get to be the General's aide, Captain? By saying things about Bill that he enjoyed hearing? (*A pause.*)

SEEGER. I choose my aide on the basis of his record, and Captain Thibaudeau has one of the finest records of any young officer on this post. His friendship with Bill had nothing to do with my decision. Your remark is an insult to him. And to me, too.

HELENA. (*Turning.*) I am not carrying a neurotic shield . . .

THIBAUDEAU. If you believe I've been speaking to please the General and stay his aide, Mrs. Seeger, I think you ought to know that I've been after him for two months to relieve me of this duty.

SEEGER. Right! He has!

THIBAUDEAU. I've cleared the path for an assignment at a post near New Orleans, where my family is and where my wife and I could live a most agreeable life. At the moment, to displease the

General would be to my distinct advantage. He'd release me a great deal more readily. Sir . . . (*Turns and goes towards door,* L.)

HELENA. Captain! (*Thibaudeau, near the door, stops and turns.*) That "very small group" of "emotionally disturbed men" who "guarded the Army's purity"; were you by any chance one of them? (*A pause.*)

SEEGER. (*Looks at Helena.*) What?

THIBAUDEAU. I most certainly was not.

SEEGER. I'm sorry, Dick. You'd better go now.

HELENA. I thought you might be. Your name is French, isn't it? Thibaudeau?

THIBAUDEAU. Yes.

HELENA. A man with a French name might be nicknamed "Froggy," mightn't he? French. Frog. Froggy. (*A pause.*)

THIBAUDEAU. I had no nickname at the Point. Except Dick, that is. I never administered any hazings beyond the usual bracings and push-ups. I never hazed Bill at all. He was my friend. We *all* liked him. Very much. (*A pause.*)

HELENA. You keep reading those psychology books, Captain. I hope you find whatever it is you're looking for. (*A beat.*)

THIBAUDEAU. I'll be at the Club, sir. (*Thibaudeau turns, opens the door, and exits, closing the door after him. Corporal rises as Thibaudeau passes through anteroom, then resumes seat in swivel chair. Seeger turns slowly to Helena.*)

HELENA. You chose your aide poorly, General.

SEEGER. You think that—he was . . . ?

HELENA. Your fine young officer has disease inside of him. Give him that release he wants; he might stand you at attention and torture it out of you!

SEEGER. You heard him deny the nickname!

HELENA. That butter-mouth could deny anything you—

SEEGER. (*Cutting in on "deny."*) No, no, I—I know him! More than an aide! His record is— No, I won't believe it. There's no evidence, only your—spite and your malice.

HELENA. This is your day for not believing, isn't it. Bill killed himself, and that aide with the glowing record bears part of the blame. Part of it. A *small* part . . . (*A beat.*)

SEEGER. Bill was not unhappy. . . .

HELENA. On the word of that impartial, disinterested witness?

40

That Galahad? (*A beat. Seeger takes up his telephone with forced decisiveness.*)

SEEGER. All right, we'll get an impartial witness in here. We'll get the final, rock-bottom truth in here! (*Into phone.*) Officers Club.

HELENA. Who?

SEEGER. Colonel Bonney. Bill's chief. He was there that morning, and saw with his own two eyes. Will *his* word cut ground with you? I'll humor this—*nightmare* of yours, and rout it, and enjoy my luncheon. . . . (*Rena enters anteroom,* L. *Corporal rises.*)

RENA. Is the General inside?

SEEGER. There are two lines at the Club; try the other. This is General Seeger, and it's important.

CORPORAL. Yes, ma'am.

(*Without knocking, Rena opens the office door and enters. A beat. Seeger hangs up the telephone. Rena closes the door behind her. Corporal resumes seat. A pause.*)

SEEGER. I told you to go with General Vohs and Mr. McKay.

RENA. I did, and when we got there, your car didn't come. Why are you back here?

SEEGER. I want you at the Club, Rena, to stand in for me. I have to—stay here a little while.

RENA. Why? What has she done? What has she said to you?

SEEGER. Nothing. Nothing at all. . . . (*A beat.*)

RENA. *What did you tell him, Helena?*

SEEGER. Nothing, Rena!

HELENA. *Bill committed suicide!* (*A pause.*)

RENA. You—*believe* her?

SEEGER. No.

RENA. (*Step* U., *towards Seeger.*) You were so—pale when you came on the platform. . . .(*To Helena.*) Have you any—proof to back up this—lie, this *hateful, fantastic lie!*

HELENA. The proof of knowing Bill, of having seen his misery, of having heard him speak suicide a dozen times.

RENA. That's not proof. . . . That's—nothing! Nothing! (*To Seeger.*) Why do you stay here? (*To Helena.*) Go home. Go home and leave us alone! You come here with lies. . . . (*Helena doesn't move. Rena turns to Seeger.*) Why do you still stay here? The telephone was in your hand. . . .

41

SEEGER. I'm going to have Colonel Bonney come over. . . .

RENA. Why . . . ?

SEEGER. To hear about that morning from his lips. For her. So that we can—*settle* this.

RENA. Settle . . . ? There's nothing *to* settle. You don't believe her. She has no proof. Only . . . bitterness . . . Bitterness and anger! (*To Helena.*) Bitterness!

HELENA. (*Step* U. R.) "A neurotic shield" is the phrase we're using today. (*A beat.*)

RENA. Will, don't . . . Don't do this. They're—expecting you at the Club. The drinks are being served and soon they'll be going into the dining room. You come back there with me. Now.

HELENA. Why don't you want him to call Bonney?

RENA. Because this day has been all planned and you want to upset it and you don't care how you do it!

HELENA. (*Turning to Rena.*) What are you afraid of?

RENA. Nothing! Nothing! I just *don't* want Will worried and upset for no good reason! It's pointless, calling people over; we've seen the official reports. . . .

HELENA. What are you hiding, Rena? How much do you know?

RENA. I'm not hiding anything! Go home! You've come here with lies!

SEEGER. Rena—

RENA. Come to the Club, Will!

SEEGER. Rena . . . if there's something you know, that you haven't told me, for God's sake . . . *tell me now.*

RENA. No. I don't know anything! I was on the ship, the same as you! I read the same cable, the same reports when we landed, the same letter from General Ramey. . . .

SEEGER. Rena—

RENA. Will, please, as a favor to me, come to the Club where you're supposed to be. Don't let her spoil things. Everyone is waiting for you. On the patio, with music . . . If it were true, wouldn't General Ramey have known? Wouldn't the records have said so? If you listen to her you're doubting the records, you're doubting General Ramey. . . . (*A beat.*)

HELENA. Call Colonel Bonney.

RENA. Will . . . please . . . (*A beat.*)

SEEGER. I have to settle this, Rena . . . I can't go to the Club, and drink, and shake hands . . . (*A pause. Hesitantly he picks up the telephone.*) Officers Club. (*A pause.*)

RENA. She's making it up. (*A pause.*)

SEEGER. This is General Seeger, Sergeant. Would you get Lieutenant Colonel Bonney to the phone. Bonney. He's probably out on the patio with the other guests. (*A pause. Seeger, Rena and Helena look at one another. The lights dim almost to blackness, and come up full on Corporal.*)

CORPORAL. (*Turning to audience.*) Colonel Bonney, the impartial witness, the rock-bottom truth . . . The ride from the Officers Club takes eight minutes; we'll contract it to one, or less than one. (*Rises, steps D. to edge of stage.*) Before, at the parade, Seeger inspected the troops. They heightened to attention by companies, and he, standing in the back of a slow-driving jeep, returned the salute of each company commander. That was mere formal inspection; there are closer, more searching ones, where a button unbuttoned can kill a weekend pass. Inspection in the Army is no less important than inspection outside the Army, where too sharp a lapel can kill a promotion, or too low a gown can kill a reputation. Now Seeger's begun a still closer inspection, searching behind the uniform. Doubt has been thrown on the Captain, his aide; we await the Lieutenant Colonel, and Seeger calls this the end, the rock-bottom. But inspection, once begun, is a rolling locomotive. I remember in basic a maniac sergeant who brandished a filthy towel and cried "Whose towel is this? The blankety-blank runs twice around the field!" And the towel, of course, was his own, and he ran twice around the field. Well once around the field, and then he forgave himself. (*Looks off L.*) And here is the Colonel. . . . (*Lights come up in office. Seeger is sitting behind the desk, wiping his palms with a handkerchief. His jacket is draped over the back of his chair. Helena stands D. R., smoking, her back to the desk. Rena sits U. L., watching Seeger. The cyclorama is a deeper blue than before. Bonney enters the anteroom.*)

BONNEY. Lieutenant Colonel Bonney to see General Seeger.

CORPORAL. Yes, sir. (*Corporal goes to door, knocks. Helena turns.*)

SEEGER. Come in. (*Corporal opens door.*)

CORPORAL. Sir, Colonel Bonney is here. (*A beat. Seeger pockets handkerchief.*)

SEEGER. Ask him to come in. (*Corporal withdraws.*)

CORPORAL. (*To Bonney.*) Sir . . . (*Bonney enters office and stands guardedly just within door. Seeger rises.*)

BONNEY. General. Mrs. Seeger. (*To Helena.*) Mrs. Seeger . . . (*Helena extinguishes her cigarette, acknowledging the greeting with a nod, her eyes on Bonney. Corporal closes the door.*)

SEEGER. I'm sorry to have taken you away from the—Club, Colonel Bonney. (*Bonney is silent.*) Will you take a seat, please? (*Corporal eases into swivel chair. Bonney advances to* C., *pulls visitor's chair to* D. L. *of desk, sits. Seeger sits. Helena sits* D. R. *on couch.*) Colonel, I would like you to describe—in detail—my son's death. (*A pause.*)

BONNEY. May I ask why?

SEEGER. I would rather not answer that now. (*A beat.*)

BONNEY. But—I've told this story half a dozen times; surely you've all seen transcripts of the record.

SEEGER. I would like you to tell it again, please. (*A beat.*)

BONNEY. The details may not be exact . . .

HELENA. After half a dozen tellings?

BONNEY. Sixteen months ago, Mrs. Seeger. That's a long time . . . (*A pause. Bonney tries to sound factual and dispassionate in his narration, but strain is evident throughout.*) We were running a series of tests on a hand grenade with an aluminum-alloy casing. The tests were conducted in a concrete-walled room lined with hanging lead sheets. The lead caught the fragments and we were able to chart their pattern and velocity.

SEEGER. The grenades were detonated . . .

BONNEY. By an arm-and-clamp device attached to a steel table in the center of the room. A grenade would be mounted on the arm, clamped, and then unpinned. The clamp kept the firing lever from springing until it was released by push-button from the control room.

SEEGER. Where was the control room?

BONNEY. Thirty, forty feet down the corridor.

SEEGER. But you could see into the testing room.

BONNEY. We had two shielded television cameras there, on a closed circuit to monitors in the control room. One gave us a close-up of the steel table with the arm-and-clamp device, and the other gave a full view of the entire room.

SEEGER. A *clear* view?

BONNEY. Absolutely clear. (*Seeger glances at Helena. She shifts*

44

noncommittally.) It was the first test of that morning. Lieutenant Seeger was in the control room, along with me and Lieutenant Parisi, the other officer on the project. The enlisted men were—

SEEGER. (*On "enlisted."*) There were other officers present, though, when Bill—at the actual time he—

BONNEY. No, just Parisi and I (*A beat.*)

SEEGER. The letter I got from General Ramey said something about "in the presence of the entire staff." (*A beat.*)

BONNEY. Well, I suppose he meant the entire staff of *that particular project,* which, aside from Bill, was—just Parisi and me. And the two enlisted men, of course. (*A beat.*)

SEEGER. Go ahead.

BONNEY. Bill and Parisi and I were in the control room. The enlisted men were in the testing room, setting up for the test. We were watching them on the monitors. Parisi had just brought in some coffee. One of the enlisted men, the Corporal, was opening the clamp on the arm. The other man, the PFC, was standing by, holding the grenade to be tested. A piece of tissue paper, part of the grenade's wrapping, was still around it. The Corporal couldn't open the clamp. It had been repaired improperly after the test of the day before and it was a little tight. The PFC put the grenade on the table and tried to help him. In the number two monitor, the close-up one, we saw the tissue paper around the grenade stretch tight and begin to tear; the firing lever had sprung away from the grenade's body. Either the pin had broken or there had never been a pin in it. Packing had kept the lever in place during shipment, and the man's hand had held it until he put the grenade down. Then the lever released. Bill said "Oh God" and ran out of the room. I pressed a button that rang a danger bell in the testing room, but the two men just looked around, not understanding how there could be any danger. Then one of them touched the grenade, rolled it back a bit, and there was the lever sticking up out of the tissue paper. They froze, and before they could come out of it, the door of the room opened and Bill burst in. He knocked them both away from the table and picked up the grenade. I suppose he was going to throw it into the corner of the room, where there was a shallow pit that would have lessened the explosion somewhat. It went off in his hand. We checked later and found a loose pin in the case of grenades. (*A pause.*)

SEEGER. Colonel . . . did Bill seem in any way—depressed that morning?

BONNEY. No, he seemed no different than he was any other morning. Cheerful . . .

HELENA. He had been deeply despondent all that past month.

BONNEY. I saw no signs of—despondency.

HELENA. Just two weeks earlier you had called him into your office, and had asked him if anything was troubling him, and had suggested that he take a few weeks' leave. (*A beat.*)

SEEGER. Is that—true?

BONNEY. I—don't remember anything like that. He was in—very good spirits. He did have some leave time coming to him, and I suggested that he take it then rather than in the summer, when we were expecting a heavy work-load. The suggestion had nothing to do with any despondency, though. The work-load is heavy in summer. (*A beat. Seeger is silent, looking at Bonney.*)

HELENA. You're a poor liar, Colonel; you ought to take lessons from the General's aide.

BONNEY. (*Rising.*) May I go, sir?

HELENA. (*Rising.*) I thought Bill's death had only been misinterpreted. Now I think it is being deliberately lied about.

BONNEY. Sir.

HELENA. I don't believe a word he's spoken! (*A beat.*)

SEEGER. Sit for a moment, Colonel.

BONNEY. I would like to get back to the—

SEEGER. (*On "get."*) Sit, Colonel. (*A beat. Bonney sits.*)

RENA. Why do you go on? (*A pause. Helena sits.*)

SEEGER. There was no speaker system, no intercom, between that control room and the testing room?

BONNEY. There was, but . . . it wasn't working. It was being rewired; it hadn't been working for several days.

SEEGER. And you went on with the testing?

BONNEY. There was no real need for an intercom. The bell was the evacuation signal in case of danger.

HELENA. Why didn't the men obey it? (*Bonney looks at Helena. No answer.*)

SEEGER. Why didn't the men obey the bell?

BONNEY. (*Looks at Seeger.*) Well, they were new men. They'd only been with us for a week or two.

SEEGER. Both of them?

BONNEY. Yes, both. Yes. I suppose they thought the bell had been sounded accidentally.

SEEGER. Didn't you question them?

BONNEY. Yes. Later, at the hospital. They said they couldn't see any danger so they thought the bell had been sounded accidentally.

SEEGER. You said you "supposed" they thought that.

BONNEY. No, that *is* what they thought. They said so. I did not come in here prepared to *testify* this way! You—you mustn't pick at my words; I'm telling the truth. . . . The men thought the bell was accidental, and then, when they saw the lever had sprung, they froze. They were inexperienced. Twenty-year-olds.

SEEGER. They'd been trained. They must have been to Munitions School.

BONNEY. They hadn't been trained enough. (*A beat.*)

SEEGER. That hand grenade, Colonel, was it different in any way from other grenades, aside from its alloy casing?

BONNEY. No, except for that, a perfectly ordinary grenade; the lever on a spring; deadly without a pin.

SEEGER. A five-second fuse?

BONNEY. Yes, a perfectly ordinary—grenade. (*A beat.*)

RENA. Why do you go on this way? (*A beat.*)

SEEGER. I go on because . . . Because it strikes me now . . . could Bill have seen the lever release, could he have run from one room, down a long corridor, and into another room, could he have picked up the grenade—all in the space of five small seconds? (*A beat.*)

BONNEY. It wasn't a—long corridor.

HELENA. Thirty or forty feet, you said!

SEEGER. Thirty feet?

BONNEY. Less . . . (*A contemptuous sound from Helena.*)

SEEGER. Much less? Twenty? That's less than the width of this office. . . .

HELENA. Say ten feet, or five! Erase the corridor completely! Erase Bill! (*A beat.*)

SEEGER. How long was the corridor, Colonel?

BONNEY. I'm not—not sure. I told you, it's hard to be exact. Sixteen months . . .

SEEGER. You're still at Colleran, still at the Weapons Testing Center. How far is it from that control room to that testing room? Today, not sixteen months ago.

47

BONNEY. Let me think. . . . (*A pause.*)

SEEGER. Colonel . . .

BONNEY. I would say . . . twenty-five feet.

HELENA. You would say.

SEEGER. It's—not impossible . . . Bill was quick. . . .

RENA. Five seconds is a long time!   BONNEY. Five seconds is longer than it sounds.

(*A beat. Seeger looks at the two of them.*)

HELENA. Five seconds is five seconds. (*A beat.*)

SEEGER. You say . . . a loose pin was found in the case of grenades.

BONNEY. That's right. . . .

SEEGER. Pins don't fall out of grenades . . . I know grenades; it takes force to pull the pin.

BONNEY. I did not say that the pin had fallen out. Maybe the grenade was packed without a pin, and the loose one was only a coincidence. Maybe the grenade had a pin in it, a broken pin. There's no way of knowing.

SEEGER. That PFC, he never noticed that the grenade he was carrying had a broken pin? Or no pin at all?

BONNEY. There was the tissue paper around the grenade.

SEEGER. And when he put the grenade on the table, he didn't feel the lever moving as his fingers left it? Even through the tissue paper? (*A beat.*)

BONNEY. Apparently not.

SEEGER. I think he would have felt it. . . .

BONNEY. He was inexperienced.

SEEGER. (*Rising.*) The spring has pressure; he would have felt it pushing. . . .

BONNEY. He was a boy, a new boy.

SEEGER. He had nerves in his fingers.

BONNEY. It was the first test he worked on! That's why we were watching so carefully!

SEEGER. You said he'd been there a week or two! Both the enlisted men!

BONNEY. No tests before that! Paper work! All week. We were doing paper work. Charts . . . (*A pause.*)

SEEGER. That clamp on the arm. It was tight because it had been repaired wrong after the test of the day before. (*A beat.*)

BONNEY. Yes, I—I did say that. Yes. There *was* a test the day

48

before. I had forgotten. But the PFC had only watched. He hadn't actually worked with the Corporal. . . . (A beat.)

SEEGER. Now you listen, Colonel . . . (Coming around desk, R.) In a little over two hours I am to dedicate a building to my son's memory, because he gave his life to save that PFC and that corporal. I need the truth from you!

BONNEY. I've told you the truth!

SEEGER. An intercom that wasn't working; is that the truth? A grenade with no pin, covered up in tissue paper; is that true? Men without experience assigned to Weapons Testing? A ten-second run made in five seconds?

BONNEY. I've told you the truth.

SEEGER. (Before Bonney now.) What have you cooked up, you and that Parisi fellow?

BONNEY. (Rising.) Sir—I'm sorry; I respect your rank, but General Ramey is my commander, and I've already violated his orders by—talking as much as I have.

SEEGER. What orders?

BONNEY. Policy. Policy at Fort Colleran—and here and at every post—to avoid discussing on-post incidents with outsiders.

SEEGER. I'm no outsider!

BONNEY. I must—go to that luncheon. . . . (Bonney turns and goes L. towards door. A beat, then Seeger rushes after him, grabs him by the shoulder, swings him around and pushes him roughly back towards C.)

SEEGER. You stay in that chair until I tell you to leave, God damn you!

RENA. Will! (Rena and Helena have risen.)

SEEGER. You sit down and remember who's the general in this room! (Bonney, white-faced, has backed clumsily into the chair under Seeger's angry advance. Rena and Helena have moved in. Helena steadies chair with one hand.)

RENA. Will, please! You musn't! You have no right to push this man and shout at him!

SEEGER. (Overlapping, starting on "push.") Get back there, Rena, and stay out of this! (Bonney casts a desperate glance at Helena, as though help might come from her direction.)

RENA. You mustn't do this!

SEEGER. Get back, do you hear me? And stay back! I want you quiet! (Unwillingly Rena retreats a few steps. Seeger turns on

49

Bonney.) Now you give me the truth of what happened that morning. Is she right; did Bill commit suicide?

BONNEY. General Ramey is my commander. I obey his orders. I always obey orders. . . . (*A beat.*)

SEEGER. Then you obey mine, you damned— What happened in that testing room? (*A pause. Bonney is silent, ashen, his eyes staring robot-like straight ahead.*) How did you get into that uniform? It's dirty with you inside it. . . . (*Seeger grabs Bonney by his lapels and uproots him from the chair.*) Open your mouth, you God-damned robot! (*Helena tries to wrest Bonney from Seeger's grip. Rena rushes forward and pulls at Seeger's arm.*)

SEEGER. *There's*	HELENA.	BONNEY.	RENA. No! Stop!
a building I'm go-	Let go! God	Let go of	Stop it! Stop! *It's*
ing to dedicate! I	Almighty,	me! Let go!	*true! It's true!*
put his name on	you're going	Please,	*He committed su-*
the list! You talk	to— Let go	you're hurt-	*icide!* It's true!
or I'll beat the	of him!	ing me!	Stop it! He com-
truth out of you!			mitted suicide. It's
Did he kill him-			true. . . .
self? Did he?			
Talk, God damn			
you! Did he? Did			
he?			

(*Rena's last few lines are in the clear, Seeger having cut short his tirade when her words finally reached him. A beat.*)

RENA. He wrote me a letter . . . the night before. . . . He wrote me . . . (*A beat. Seeger releases Bonney, who sits weakly. All eyes on Rena.*)

SEEGER. A letter . . . ?

RENA. It was waiting for me, when we came off the ship. . . .

HELENA. You've known, too, all along. . . .

SEEGER. Where? Let me see it. Where is it?

RENA. Burned. I burned it, in the cellar. (*A beat.*)

SEEGER. What did he say?

RENA. I—don't remember. Good-bye, forgive me. . . . He didn't blame anyone . . .

SEEGER. *What were his words?*

RENA. I forget! (*A beat.*)

SEEGER. You're lying. You wouldn't forget a letter like that. No one would. There *was* no letter. It's a lie. Another one of her afternoon stories. Burned in the cellar! What afternoon did you see that? It's a lie, to get my hands off this God-damned— (*To Bonney.*) —liar! (*To Helena.*) Liar! (*To Rena.*) *Liar!* Liars, every one of you. . . . (*To the heavens, thunderously.*) *LIARS!* (*A beat.*)

RENA. (*Her eyes on Seeger.*) "Dear Mother. . . . At last I have made one decision in this life of mine. By the time you read this you will know what the decision was. I don't want you to mourn me too long, Mother, and I don't want you to blame yourself for anything that's happened. I don't want Papa and Helena to blame themselves, either, but even on paper I haven't got guts enough to face them. I've disappointed them so much." (*A beat.*)

BONNEY. He intercepted the enlisted men on the way to the testing room. "Give me the grenade," he said. "I'll set it up. You boys go have yourselves a smoke." They smelled—liquor on him, but they gave him the grenade, because he was an officer. (NOTE: *throughout this passage no attempt is made to blueprint Seeger's reactions. The throat-sounds of disbelief and of pain, the helpless turnings from one attacked flank to the other, these are for the actor and director to create between them. The overall effect, from the thunderous "Liars!" to the anguished "Oh God . . . !" should be of a towering bull being brought to its knees by picadors on either side.*)

RENA. "I can't go on, Mother. You and Papa are coming back from Europe and he is going to have me assigned to his new post. He wonders when I am going to make Captain in every one of those two-a-week letters of his, and now he is going to *help me* make Captain, and Major, and whatever else there is in this pointless, endless parade we're in. I'm so goddam *tired,* Mother . . . (*A beat.*)

BONNEY. He came into the testing room. We saw him on the monitor. Parisi turned on the intercom. "Where are the boys, Bill?" He didn't answer. He just went over to the table and stood there with the grenade in his hand. "Bill, what's the matter?"

RENA. "And then there's Helena. Now that she's expecting, I know she'll stay with me for the baby's sake. That's wrong; she should have left me long ago. She should have admitted she picked the wrong man instead of trying to make me into the right one. She's a tough giver-upper, though. She deserves someone a hundred times better than I am. I never realized it until this minute, but she and Papa are very much alike. They're strong, and they expect so much of themselves and of everybody else. I love them, Mother. If I didn't, I suppose I wouldn't hate myself so." (*A beat.*)

BONNEY. He pulled the pin out of the grenade and laid the grenade on the table and leaned over the table with his eyes closed and his hands gripping the far edge of it. We shouted into the intercom and rang the danger bell. The enlisted men had been watching through the port in the door. They ran in and tried to pull him away from the table. He hung on.

RENA. "Good-bye, Mother, and forgive me. I know you will. I love you most of all, because you never expected me to be anything I wasn't. William."

BONNEY. They kept pulling at him. He turned and knocked them away—madman strength!—then turned again and flung himself across the table. At the very last second. (*A beat.*)

RENA. His handwriting was so neat and small and fine. . . . It never changed. . . . (*A pause. There are tears on Rena's face. Helena, also crying, turns away. Seeger stands shakenly between Bonney and Rena.*)

SEEGER. Oh, God . . . ! Why did you keep it from me? Why did you burn it?

RENA. He was dead; you were alive.

SEEGER. (*Turning to Bonney.*) Flung himself, you said, on top of the—table. . . . (*Bonney nods. Helena sits on couch D. R. Seeger turns again to Rena.*) You let me put his name on the list. . . .

RENA. Could I have stopped you, without telling you?

SEEGER. Oh, God . . . (*Turning away.*) I thought I knew him . . . I thought he was . . . me. . . . Eighteenth out of four hundred and nine . . . I thought he was me. . . . (*He strikes himself. A pause. He catches the edge of the desk, holds it to force himself forward.*) Why did you lie? Liar! *Why did you lie?*

BONNEY. I was given orders; I obeyed them. My life is—obeying orders.

SEEGER. Ramey's orders? (*A beat.*)

BONNEY. I called him. "Speak to no one," he said. "Get over here, quickly." In his office, later, we . . . made our story. Facts and photographs had already been gathered and were beginning to leak. We fit the story to them. Parisi and the enlisted men were . . . ordered to agree.

SEEGER. Why? To keep clean his precious Fort Colleran? (*Bonney is silent.*) He'll pay for this, I swear he will! And stuck to his lie when the dedication was announced; hid himself away, knowing what he knew! He'll pay before a court-martial! You tell him I swear to that! I wanted . . . such good things for him. . . . Get out! Go straight to General Ramey and tell him what's coming. There's no dedication you have to stay for.

BONNEY. (*Rising.*) You're stopping it? (*A beat. Helena looks up.*)

SEEGER. Yes. . . . Yes. I'm stopping it. Dedications—aren't for men who've been—pushed into dying. . . . (*A beat. Rena turns u., wiping her eyes. Bonney goes L. to the door. He stops with his hand on the knob.*)

BONNEY. Are you sure you'll be able to stop it?

SEEGER. Of course. What do you mean? (*A beat.*)

BONNEY. Perhaps you and I belong to different armies. . . . (*Bonney exits, closing the door after him. Corporal rises as Bonney passes through anteroom, then resumes seat.*)

SEEGER. Different armies? . . . He's—crazy, talking like that. . . . I'll get them here and tell them. Mr. McKay and General Vohs. They'll *order* me to stop the dedication!

RENA. (*Turning.*) Will they?

SEEGER. Of course they will! I *know* their kind of men!

RENA. No, you don't, Will. You never have. You're blind with love. That's why you've gone as high as you have, but no higher. Love-blind people are useful for running the training camps, but they get in the way where decisions are being made. You've only been in the Army thirty-nine years; I've been in it all my life.

SEEGER. This—isn't *you*, Rena.

RENA. (*Without rancor; almost tenderly.*) Oh, Will, how would you know what's me and what isn't me? (*She goes u. for her handbag. Seeger watches her dumbly.*) I'm going home. I don't care whether the building is dedicated to Bill or not. (*Seeger stares at her. With her handbag tucked under her arm, she begins putting on, with difficulty, a pair of small white gloves. The tears are in her eyes again.*) He loved me most of all. Did you see that? Hear me read that? And I was the one who hurt him most of all.

SEEGER. You—

RENA. By letting you do what you did to him. I had eyes, but I closed them. I chose your happiness over his.

SEEGER. You *wanted* him in the Army . . .

RENA. I wanted what you wanted; that's all I've *ever* wanted.

53

You handed him to your Army—yes, yours, not mine—but I handed him to you. (*Trying to smile.*) *You're* my Army. You're selfish, and overbearing, and thoughtless and stubborn. All you care about is following your own map, regardless of how the people with you are tripping and getting hurt. And I love you. That is the mystery of my life. I'm fifty-four; sometimes I think I must be mad to love you the—honeymoon way I do. I'm going home now. I'm going to pull the blinds in the living room, and put on my green bathrobe, and turn on the television set, and sit and watch. Don't make fun of me any more, Will. Please. It hurts me very much. (*Rena exits L., leaving the door open. Corporal rises as Rena passes through anteroom, then remains standing, facing office. Helena rises. Seeger makes a move to follow Rena, then stops.*)

SEEGER. Oh my God . . . (*Turning.*) Where do I begin to—comfort her?

HELENA. I don't know. . . .

SEEGER. (*Looking off again.*) I've buried her alive. . . . (*Turning.*) And buried Bill dead. . . .

HELENA. I helped you there. It took the two of us, pulling two ways, to break him. (*Seeger and Helena look at each other, their first unarmed moment.*) He knew us well. Alike, he said . . . I'm more your child than he was. (*A beat.*)

SEEGER. He was wrong, though, about—other things. And so is Rena, and Bonney. I'll show you. (*Helena moves up, stands near Seeger. His hand is on the telephone.*) Sure, in the Army's lower levels you can find some—weakness, and deceit, and—selfishness. That's human! You'll find that in anybody, in any organization. My God, I don't say it's lily-white! But at the top, when the chips are down, it's—different. There's a system, and there's right, and there's—honor. I *know* that.

HELENA. I—hope so. I do. . . . (*Recognizing the truth of what she is saying.*) I do hope . . . ! (*A beat. Seeger raises the receiver.*)

SEEGER. Officers Club. Please. (*He wipes his hand over his mouth, stays it on his cheek.*) This morning, shaving, I smiled in the mirror. . . . (*The lights fade to total blackness, simultaneously coming up on Corporal. He is standing. He turns to the audience.*)

CORPORAL. The day is finding its final shape now. Boyd McKay, the Assistant Secretary of the Army, and General Vohs, the Deputy

54

Commanding General of the First Army, make an unobtrusive exit from the Officers Club. In an olive-drab sedan, with an enlisted man at the wheel and a chromium star on the front bumper, they drive this way. Passing soldiers salute them. Now I claim the playwright's ancient privilege of basing one broad statement on the particulars of the play's action. Bear with me, please. An Army is, like all societies, made of men, and men are made of—scientists know what; phosphates and sulfates; you've heard it before; we function as we can, bend with the breeze, turn with the tide, build our puny campfires and elbow and gouge for the nearest, safest place. And so on. And then comes a man like Seeger, who sees heaven on this earth, and tramples us in his pursuit of it. We don't like him much; it's *good* to see his eyes forced open; he, with his complacency of system and honor and goodness and right, crashing along, while we, with our toes trodden, are slapped with extra drill on Saturday afternoon because the Captain is trying every which way to make Major! There's your system and honor and goodness and right. But here is the statement; agree or disagree; heaven begins in the eye of a human. No dome was ever raised without walls to support it, no walls ever erected without foundations to hold them, no foundations ever laid without the ground being cleared to receive them. And who begins the clearing of the ground? One man, maybe mad, who has seen in the air the outline of a shimmering dome. We'll go on with the play now. Seeger, with Vohs and McKay . . . (*Lights come up full in office and fade to half on Corporal. Cyclorama is a deep empurpled blue. Seeger, with his jacket on and carefully buttoned, stands behind the desk. Vohs sits* D. R. *of desk; McKay sits* D. L. *of desk. Helena sits near Seeger,* U. R. *The door is closed. Corporal eases into swivel chair. Seeger wipes his palms inconspicuously on his trouser sides.*)

SEEGER. Gentlemen . . . I've learned a—terrible truth, here in this office, since the parade. My son's death was—not the heroism described in the official report. It was—an act of suicide. The enlisted men were injured trying to save *him*. (*A pause. Vohs and McKay look at one another.*)

VOHS. Are you certain of this?

SEEGER. Would I say it if I weren't certain? My wife received a letter; he made his intention plain. She burned the letter, out of—concern for me. It was I who—pushed him. . . . Lieutenant Colonel Bonney has admitted the entire truth. General Ramey con-

cealed the truth to keep a black mark off Fort Colleran. Mr. Mc-
Kay, I urge you as strongly as I can to bring him to account for
his—disgraceful act. He shames his uniform. Bonney was his part-
ner in the lie, but Bonney's only fault was obedience. Which I
never knew till now could *be* a fault. . . . In light of all this . . .
I am going to call Troop Command and give orders for the dis-
missal of the troops and the cancellation of the dedication ceremony. (*Vohs' and McKay's eyes meet again.*) The Recreation
Center will stay undedicated until you and your superiors have
had a chance to choose a—more fitting recipient for the honor,
although I *would* like to let the men go ahead with the—dance
they've planned there for this evening. I thought it proper to inform
you of this before calling Colonel Parmalee, the Troop Commander.
(*A pause. Vohs and McKay are still in mute conference. Seeger
watches them, and reaches slowly for the telephone.*)
MCKAY. One moment, please, General . . . (*A beat. Seeger's
fingertips are on the receiver.*)
SEEGER. Mr. McKay . . .
MCKAY. The ceremony should, of course, be stopped, and another recipient chosen for the dedication. Your willingness to call
Colonel Parmalee, considering the—public embarrassment that
might result for you and your wife . . . and your daughter-in-law
. . . reflects well on your integrity and your respect for the significance of the honor. The ceremony should be stopped. There
would be no question at all about it, if the significance of the honor
were the only factor involved. (*A pause.*)
SEEGER. There's . . . another factor . . . ?
MCKAY. There is. Yes, there is. . . . (*A beat. Helena shifts forward.*) A building such as this recreation center serves a dual function; you must be aware of that. Its first function is the objective
one of giving the enlisted men recreational facilities. Its second
function, less objective but no less important, lies in the area of—
public relations. This is not a pleasant area for men like us to work
in, but it's one in which we *must* work so long as this country is
a democracy and not a dictatorship. We must create a favorable
image of the Army in the mind of the public; we must gain the
approval which is given us in war and denied us the day after the
victory; we must win, finally, the *appropriations* that are essential
to the defense of the very people who would withhold those appropriations. To achieve all this we must rely on a program of public

persuasion, public relations. Impressive recreation centers for the enlisted men are a part of that program. The ceremony dedicating such a building, therefore, also serves two purposes. One, it honors a man and puts a name on the building, and two, it *points attention to the building*, so that the building can perform to the fullest its public relations function.

SEEGER. And you feel that this—second purpose of a dedication is—as important as its first purpose. . . .

MCKAY. Ultimately, I feel that it is more important. (*A beat.*)

SEEGER. You want the ceremony to go on.

MCKAY. I do, and I believe General Vohs will agree with me. (*A beat. Vohs nods.*) Your Public Information Office and First Army's P.I.O. have created a considerable amount of interest in the event. Changing the recipient of the dedication could not be explained in any way that wouldn't bring bad publicity rather than good. We regret as much as you do the necessity to take a less than honest course, particularly when it's your own son who's involved, but you must bear in mind that the Army's final mission is not to dispense honors with justice; it is to defend this country; that is our single purpose.

SEEGER. The final mission . . . the end; that's what counts. . . .

MCKAY. Yes.

SEEGER. (*Turning part way towards Helena.*) And the end is I made him a soldier. . . . (*A beat.*)

MCKAY. I beg your pardon?

SEEGER. Don't you think the—way the mission is accomplished counts, too? An honor for heroes shouldn't be made into a—tool for public relations.

MCKAY. It's past one-thirty, General; a bit late for arguing the-ends-and-the-means. In the circumstances, you will not be expected to perform the dedication yourself. The Brigadier who commands your Ordnance Schools . . .

VOHS. Timmerman.

MCKAY. General Timmerman will stand in for you at the ceremony. We'll tell the reporters that you've been taken ill. One of them remarked on your paleness on the platform, so the story should hold water. Would you call General Timmerman, please? (*Seeger stares at McKay disbelievingly.*) Would you get General Timmerman here, please? He'll have to prepare a speech.

SEEGER. You aren't the Secretary, you're his assistant. And you're not General Del Ruth; you're his deputy. I don't believe that either the Secretary or General Del Ruth would feel about this the way you men feel.

MCKAY. I assure you they would. (*A beat.*)

SEEGER. We'll see. We'll just see. . . . (*Takes up telephone.*)

MCKAY. What are you—

SEEGER. Put me on the Governors Island trunk line.

MCKAY. (*Rising.*) You won't reach General Del Ruth!

SEEGER. We'll see about that. . . .

VOHS. He's not on the Island.

MCKAY. You're wasting your time! And *our* time as well!

VOHS. (*Rising.*) He won't speak to you, Seeger. Hang up. . . .

SEEGER. Headquarters, please.

VOHS. Hang up, Seeger!

MCKAY. He knows your son killed himself! He knows. . . . And the Secretary knows, too.

SEEGER. (*Lowering the receiver.*) What—?

VOHS. We've *all* known, since the day it happened. . . . (*A beat.*)

HELENA. Oh, no . . . ! (*The receiver clicks in Seeger's hand. He hangs it up, missing the cradle once.*)

SEEGER. You've—known—?

MCKAY. Did you truly believe that Ramey took it on his own authority to issue a false report? (*Seeger lowers himself into his chair, staring at McKay. Vohs sits. McKay remains standing.*) Another officer had committed suicide five days earlier, at Fort Bliss. Word of a second suicide, within so short a period, would have been disastrous, not only in terms of outside reaction, but disastrous to morale within the Officer Corps itself. Ramey was given orders. He obeyed them.

SEEGER. (*A hand over his eyes.*) Oh, my God . . . my . . . (*Lowering hand.*) This is why Del Ruth couldn't—couldn't face coming . . . ! Why the—Secretary isn't here, either . . . ! Wait, wait, I'm lost now. You *knew* Bill committed suicide, and—still you—chose him for the dedication? (*A beat.*)

MCKAY. His name was submitted. We went by the record.

SEEGER. The record was a lie. . . . (*A beat.*)

MCKAY. We were obligated to study the records of all men submitted. . . .

SEEGER. *You knew his record was a lie! Your lie!*

58

MCKAY. Yes, God damn it, we knew! I told you, didn't I? This is a public relations project! Don't you know why those reporters are here today? Don't you know why your P.I.O. had such an easy time stirring interest in this dedication?

SEEGER. A high honor's being given. . . . A fine building . . .

MCKAY. (*Turning away.*) Oh, God!

SEEGER. They're here because they think Bill was a hero. . . .

MCKAY. (*Turning to him.*) The interest in this dedication is *human* interest! You're his father! A father is dedicating a building to his son! That's why they're here! Do you think those reporters or their readers give a *damn* about Army honors? *Sentiment* is what attracts them!

SEEGER. That's why—you chose Bill, knowing the truth about him? Because he was my son? For human interest?

MCKAY. Because he was your son. Because when something useful is handed to us we have to use it. Because we don't get handed much that's useful. We haven't yet learned the secret of spinning gold out of thin air. (*A pause.*)

SEEGER. Where did I—put my life? What uniform is this? What army am I in?

MCKAY. The Human Army! What did you *think* you were in? The Celestial Army of Sweet Jesus? Angels on parade?

SEEGER. You're *less* than human!

MCKAY. We're no better and no worse than you are! Maybe *we've* used *you*, didn't *you* use your *son*? Any wrongs we've done, you've done, too! We're you, no better and no worse!

SEEGER. I've never done wrong knowing I was doing it!

MCKAY. Life has been easy on you! I've never done wrong *without* knowing I was doing it! Don't think your ignorance constitutes virtue, though; it only constitutes ignorance!

VOHS. Boyd—

MCKAY. I'm sorry, but I am up to here with innocent baby-eyes looking at me as if I were— I had a law practice, General, a profitable one, and I gave it up because I thought there was a useful, clean job I could do, because *I* had innocent baby-eyes, too, once upon a time. Well, I spent three damned years on my knees in front of appropriations committees and got nothing each day except a bad temper to take home and lash my wife with, and then I grew some scales over my big baby-eyes and faced up to the truth of this world; it's hostile to us, this ball we're on, and you can't grow

59

anything green without shoving your hands wrist-deep into dirt and mud and manure. I've acknowledged my membership in the Grand Human Army of The Filthy Hand; I buy drinks for the committeemen and kiss their behinds when I can, I order bronze plaques with convenient lies inscribed on them, and I sub for the Secretary when he's too sick of the smell of *his* filthy hands, and we hope, both of us, all of us, that some day something green will grow. And we are up to here with people like you, the *ignorant* ones with their imaginary gloves on, staring at us as if we were Judas Iscariot. How clean are your own hands, General? Now call Timmerman and get him here to learn a speech. The reporters will be disappointed but they'll file their stories anyway, now that they've come. (*A pause.*)

SEEGER. I can't allow this to happen. . . . (*Rising.*) I'm the Commander of this post. (*A beat.*)

MCKAY. In this desk somewhere, there is a paper addressed to you and signed by General Del Ruth. It does not say the building *may* be dedicated to Lieutenant William J. Seeger, Junior; it says the building *will* be dedicated to Lieutenant William J. Seeger, Junior. It is an order, not a grant of permission. (*A beat. Seeger looks about as though at a new and foundationless world.*)

SEEGER. It's an order . . . that I—won't obey. . . . (*A pause.*)

VOHS. Seeger, believe me, I'm your friend. It's impossible for you to stop this dedication. If you try, you will—hurt yourself, very much. (*A beat.*)

HELENA. Suppose we tell the reporters the truth about Bill?

MCKAY. Have you any proof to give them? Bonney won't talk again, you can be sure of that. Nor will anyone else. And the penalty for unauthorized statements to the press can be truly grave, as the General knows. You will prove nothing. The record will stand. Your husband is dead, Mrs. Seeger; you seem intelligent; do you honestly believe it matters what words appear on a plaque, on a glorified gymnasium, on a class B military establishment? The plaque is only bronze; it will last much less than eternity.

SEEGER. It *does* matter. If it doesn't, I might as well have died when I joined up! Thirty-nine years of service I've given you! Butchered my son! And buried my wife alive! It *has* to matter!

MCKAY. All right, General. Cards on the table, and the Secretary stands behind me. The soldier who disobeys an order is relieved of his duty and the order is carried out by the man who succeeds him. That is the meaning of the word "army." If you deliberately disobey Del Ruth's order, you will be relieved of this command and the order will be carried out by someone else tomorrow or Monday. In that event, your elevation to permanent Major General will become extremely unlikely. Stars are given for service, not opposition. Now you know the price of what you're buying. (*A pause. Seeger stands as if at the rim of a cliff. Helena rises, moves to Seeger's side. He turns toward her.*)

HELENA. I don't know what to call you when I'm not saying "General" mockingly. . . . Father . . . he's right; Bill is dead, and the plaque is only bronze. I came here with a neurotic shield; there was even some truth in that aide of yours. I had neurotic arrows, too, and now that I've drawn blood, I've lost heart. Or *found* heart, maybe. Let them do it their way. Don't hurt yourself on Bill's account, or mine. Bill's beyond knowing, and even if he weren't, he would say, too, "Let them do it." You don't owe him this. Neither of us owes him anything, except sorrow. (*A pause. Seeger touches Helena's cheek, considers for a moment, and moves to the telephone. He picks it up.*)

SEEGER. Troop Command, please.

MCKAY. Put down that phone.

SEEGER. I'm the commander of this post. There will be no dedication.

VOHS. (*Rising.*) Boyd, you have no authority to stop him.

SEEGER. Colonel Parmalee, please. General Seeger.

MCKAY. Please don't do this. . . .

SEEGER. Colonel? This is Seeger. I am calling off the dedication ceremony. I want the troops dismissed. Immediately. Yes, I did. And I also want the stands in front of the Recreation Center to be taken away. Station a man there to tell people the ceremony is cancelled. The dance can go on as scheduled, but the plaque outside the building is not to be uncovered. No, there is no explanation; just these orders. Obey them, please. (*He hangs up.*)

MCKAY. (*To Vohs.*) Get to a phone, an outside phone, and call Del Ruth. I'll catch the reporters before they leave the Club. (*To Seeger.*) You haven't cancelled the dedication, General; you've postponed it for a day or two.

SEEGER. If anyone, *anyone*, dedicates that building in my son's name, I will *make* an unauthorized statement to the press, regardless of the penalty. There will be publicity even if there is no proof. (*A beat.*)

MCKAY. You've committed suicide, as surely as your son did. (*McKay exits. As he passes through anteroom Corporal rises and remains standing.*)

VOHS. I'll try to soften Del Ruth. Expect no miracles, though; McKay and the Secretary hold the power. (*Vohs exits. When he has passed through the anteroom, Corporal resumes his seat. Helena has moved* D. R. *after McKay's exit. Seeger still stands behind the desk. They look at one another. A pause.*)

SEEGER. It's true; there'll be no miracles. I disobeyed. They'll snap me in two.

HELENA. They ought to—shine your shoes.

SEEGER. No, no, no. . . . They're the ones who put me here. . . . Will you stay a while?

HELENA. I can't. . . . There's Billy. . . . If I make it to the airport by three, I can feed him his breakfast. He's cranky in the morning.

SEEGER. I'll drive you to the plane. . . .

HELENA. Rena's at home, alone. . . .

SEEGER. Yes. . . . (*A beat. Helena turns and goes to the couch for her belongings.*) Helena . . . I—loved Bill. . . .

HELENA. (*A pause, and a letting-go.*) I know you did. . . .

SEEGER. You did, too. (*A beat.*)

HELENA. Will you visit us?

SEEGER. Can we?

HELENA. (*Turning to him, smiling.*) Yes. Please. . . . (*Lights fade to half and come up full on Corporal seated in swivel chair. During the following, Helena slowly picks up her purse and satchel, and exits,* L., *looking back at Seeger. He watches her go, then pockets a few things from his desk drawer, picks up his cap, and moves* D. *of desk.*)

CORPORAL. (*Turning to audience.*) On the following Monday morning, General Seeger was ordered to Walter Reed Hospital in Washington, for a routine physical check-up. This had the effect of placing him on sick-leave, and in his absence command of the post was assumed by Brigadier General Paul Timmerman, the Commander of the Ordnance School. (*Rising and moving* D. C.) A week later Seeger returned, but he was still carried on sick-leave and did not appear in Headquarters Building. Timmerman retained command. At the end of the month, General Seeger was retired from active military duty in the permanent rank of Brigadier General; one star. Retired, he went with his wife to San Francisco, and there, fourteen months later, he died of a coronary thrombosis. I saw his obituary over my good civilian coffee one morning. He was fifty-eight. He was survived by his wife, his daughter-in-law, and his grandson. The Recreation Center was never dedicated to anyone. It slipped gradually into use, and one day the curtain and plaque were gone from beside its entrance. Where the plaque had been there were only four small pock-marks, as though four bullets had been fired from a distance against the stone. I revisited the post two months ago. The pock-marks are still there.

SEEGER. Corporal. (*Lights come up in office.*)

CORPORAL. (*Turning* u.) Sir?

SEEGER. I'd like you to stay here for a few minutes. . . . (*Coming* D.) I'll send someone to relieve you. Calls will be coming in; from Governors Island, maybe from Washington. Tell whoever calls that I've gone home and can be reached there.

CORPORAL. Yes, sir. (*A beat.*)

SEEGER. (*The cap turning in his hands.*) I guess there's . . . nothing else. . . . (*A beat. He turns and starts* L. *toward door. Corporal comes to attention and salutes.*)

CORPORAL. Sir. (*Seeger turns. Corporal holds the salute.*)

SEEGER. Oh. (*Distractedly he returns the salute. Corporal drops his arm. Seeger exits. THE CURTAIN FALLS.*)

THE END

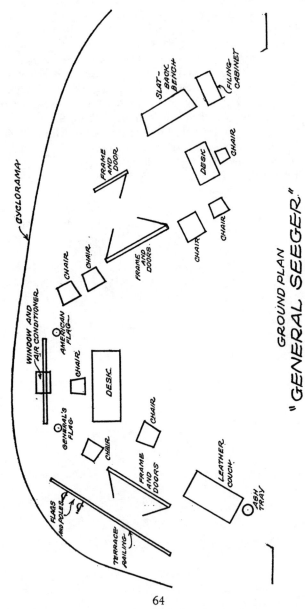

GROUND PLAN
"GENERAL SEEGER"

PROPERTY LIST

FOR GENERAL'S OFFICE

Furniture:

1 Desk—stenographer's pull-out shelf—on castors
1 Swivel arm chair on castors
5 Straight back side chairs (4 leather, 1 wooden)
2 Flag pole stands
1 Air conditioning unit, in window
2 Flags with spears (American flag and Major General's flag)
1 Pair of curtains for each side of window
1 Venetian blind
1 Lock, on the u. half of the double doors R.
1 Floor bolt on the D. half of the double doors R.
1 Portrait frame
1 Leather couch
1 Standing ash tray
1 Small table

On Desk:

1 Blotter
1 Pen and ink stand
1 Incoming-Outgoing mail tray
2 Telephones
1 Water carafe and glass on tray
1 Humidor with cigars
1 Ash tray
1 Waste paper basket
Matches

FOR ANTEROOM

Furniture:

1 Small secretarial desk
1 Small swivel chair—no arms—on castors
1 Filing cabinet
1 Bench—open slat back—with pad

On Desk:

1 Blotter
1 Pen and ink stand
1 Incoming-Outgoing mail tray
1 Ash tray
1 Phone
1 Clip board, with pencil attached
1 Waste paper basket

For Cabinet:

Files to fill one drawer
1 Feather duster

HAND PROPERTIES

1 Arm band, with "P.I.O." lettered on it (Corporal)
1 Flight bag (Helena)
1 Pint sized whiskey bottle (full), with screw top (Helena)
2 Cameras (1 small, for taking candids)
        (1 regular camera used by newsphotographers—with
          supply bag)
4 Assorted notebooks (Reporters)
1 Information card (3" x 5") (Capt. Peck)
6 Men's handkerchiefs (Gen. Seeger)
1 Pistol (Color Guards)
1 Key ring, with keys (Gen. Seeger)
1 Wristwatch (Capt. Peck)
Cigarette holder ⎱
Lighter   ⎰ (McKay)
Case
1 Clipboard, with papers (Corporal)
Purse, with cigarettes and matches (Helena)
Man's handkerchief (Helena) (Act II)
Cigarettes and matches (Corporal)

NEW PLAYS

★ **THE CIDER HOUSE RULES, PARTS 1 & 2 by Peter Parnell, adapted from the novel by John Irving.** Spanning eight decades of American life, this adaptation from the Irving novel tells the story of Dr. Wilbur Larch, founder of the St. Cloud's, Maine orphanage and hospital, and of the complex father-son relationship he develops with the young orphan Homer Wells. "...luxurious digressions, confident pacing...an enterprise of scope and vigor..." *–NY Times.* "...The fact that I can't wait to see Part 2 only begins to suggest just how good it is..." *–NY Daily News.* "...engrossing...an odyssey that has only one major shortcoming: It comes to an end." *–Seattle Times.* "...outstanding...captures the humor, the humility...of Irving's 588-page novel..." *–Seattle Post-Intelligencer.* [9M, 10W, doubling, flexible casting] PART 1 ISBN: 0-8222-1725-2 PART 2 ISBN: 0-8222-1726-0

★ **TEN UNKNOWNS by Jon Robin Baitz.** An iconoclastic American painter in his seventies has his life turned upside down by an art dealer and his ex-boyfriend. "...breadth and complexity...a sweet and delicate harmony rises from the four cast members...Mr. Baitz is without peer among his contemporaries in creating dialogue that spontaneously conveys a character's social context and moral limitations..." *–NY Times.* "...darkly funny, brilliantly desperate comedy...TEN UNKNOWNS vibrates with vital voices." *–NY Post.* [3M, 1W] ISBN: 0-8222-1826-7

★ **BOOK OF DAYS by Lanford Wilson.** A small-town actress playing St. Joan struggles to expose a murder. "...[Wilson's] best work since *Fifth of July*...An intriguing, prismatic and thoroughly engrossing depiction of contemporary small-town life with a murder mystery at its core...a splendid evening of theater..." *–Variety.* "...fascinating...a densely populated, unpredictable little world." *–St. Louis Post-Dispatch.* [6M, 5W] ISBN: 0-8222-1767-8

★ **THE SYRINGA TREE by Pamela Gien.** Winner of the 2001 Obie Award. A breathtakingly beautiful tale of growing up white in apartheid South Africa. "Instantly engaging, exotic, complex, deeply shocking...a thoroughly persuasive transport to a time and a place...stun[s] with the power of a gut punch..." *–NY Times.* "Astonishing...affecting ...[with] a dramatic and heartbreaking conclusion...A deceptive sweet simplicity haunts THE SYRINGA TREE..." *–A.P.* [1W (or flexible cast)] ISBN: 0-8222-1792-9

★ **COYOTE ON A FENCE by Bruce Graham.** An emotionally riveting look at capital punishment. "The language is as precise as it is profane, provoking both troubling thought and the occasional cheerful laugh...will change you a little before it lets go of you." *–Cincinnati CityBeat.* "...excellent theater in every way..." *–Philadelphia City Paper.* [3M, 1W] ISBN: 0-8222-1738-4

★ **THE PLAY ABOUT THE BABY by Edward Albee.** Concerns a young couple who have just had a baby and the strange turn of events that transpire when they are visited by an older man and woman. "An invaluable self-portrait of sorts from one of the few genuinely great living American dramatists...rockets into that special corner of theater heaven where words shoot off like fireworks into dazzling patterns and hues." *–NY Times.* "An exhilarating, wicked...emotional terrorism." *–NY Newsday.* [2M, 2W] ISBN: 0-8222-1814-3

★ **FORCE CONTINUUM by Kia Corthron.** Tensions among black and white police officers and the neighborhoods they serve form the backdrop of this discomfiting look at life in the inner city. "The creator of this intense...new play is a singular voice among American playwrights...exceptionally eloquent..." *–NY Times.* "...a rich subject and a wise attitude." *–NY Post.* [6M, 2W, 1 boy] ISBN: 0-8222-1817-8

DRAMATISTS PLAY SERVICE, INC.
440 Park Avenue South, New York, NY 10016 212-683-8960 Fax 212-213-1539
postmaster@dramatists.com   www.dramatists.com

NEW PLAYS

★ **A LESSON BEFORE DYING by Romulus Linney, based on the novel by Ernest J. Gaines.** An innocent young man is condemned to death in backwoods Louisiana and must learn to die with dignity. "The story's wrenching power lies not in its outrage but in the almost inexplicable grace the characters must muster as their only resistance to being treated like lesser beings." –*The New Yorker.* "Irresistable momentum and a cathartic explosion...a powerful inevitability." –*NY Times.* [5M, 2W] ISBN: 0-8222-1785-6

★ **BOOM TOWN by Jeff Daniels.** A searing drama mixing small-town love, politics and the consequences of betrayal. "...a brutally honest, contemporary foray into classic themes, exploring what moves people to lie, cheat, love and dream. By BOOM TOWN's climactic end there are no secrets, only bare truth." –*Oakland Press.* "...some of the most electrifying writing Daniels has ever done..." –*Ann Arbor News.* [2M, 1W] ISBN: 0-8222-1760-0

★ **INCORRUPTIBLE by Michael Hollinger.** When a motley order of medieval monks learns their patron saint no longer works miracles, a larcenous, one-eyed minstrel shows them an outrageous new way to pay old debts. "A lightning-fast farce, rich in both verbal and physical humor." –*American Theatre.* "Everything fits snugly in this funny, endearing black comedy...an artful blend of the mock-formal and the anachronistically breezy...A piece of remarkably dexterous craftsmanship." –*Philadelphia Inquirer.* "A farcical romp, scintillating and irreverent." –*Philadelphia Weekly.* [5M, 3W] ISBN: 0-8222-1787-2

★ **CELLINI by John Patrick Shanley.** Chronicles the life of the original "Renaissance Man," Benvenuto Cellini, the sixteenth-century Italian sculptor and man-about-town. Adapted from the autobiography of Benvenuto Cellini, translated by J. Addington Symonds. "[Shanley] has created a convincing Cellini, not neglecting his dark side, and a trim, vigorous, fast-moving show." –*BackStage.* "Very entertaining...With brave purpose, the narrative undermines chronology before untangling it...touching and funny..." –*NY Times.* [7M, 2W (doubling)] ISBN: 0-8222-1808-9

★ **PRAYING FOR RAIN by Robert Vaughan.** Examines a burst of fatal violence and its aftermath in a suburban high school. "Thought provoking and compelling." –*Denver Post.* "Vaughan's powerful drama offers hope and possibilities." –*Theatre.com.* "[The play] doesn't put forth compact, tidy answers to the problem of youth violence. What it does offer is a compelling exploration of the forces that influence an individual's choices, and of the proverbial lifelines—be they familial, communal, religious or political—that tragically slacken when society gives in to apathy, fear and self-doubt..." –*Westword.* "...a symphony of anger..." –*Gazette Telegraph.* [4M, 3W] ISBN: 0-8222-1807-0

★ **GOD'S MAN IN TEXAS by David Rambo.** When a young pastor takes over one of the most prestigious Baptist churches from a rip-roaring old preacher-entrepreneur, all hell breaks loose. "...the pick of the litter of all the works at the Humana Festival..." –*Providence Journal.* "...a wealth of both drama and comedy in the struggle for power..." –*LA Times.* "...the first act is so funny...deepens in the second act into a sobering portrait of fear, hope and self-delusion..." –*Columbus Dispatch.* [3M] ISBN: 0-8222-1801-1

★ **JESUS HOPPED THE 'A' TRAIN by Stephen Adly Guirgis.** A probing, intense portrait of lives behind bars at Rikers Island. "...fire-breathing...whenever it appears that JESUS is settling into familiar territory, it slides right beneath expectations into another, fresher direction. It has the courage of its intellectual restlessness...[JESUS HOPPED THE 'A' TRAIN] has been written in flame." –*NY Times.* [4M, 1W] ISBN: 0-8222-1799-6

DRAMATISTS PLAY SERVICE, INC.
440 Park Avenue South, New York, NY 10016 212-683-8960 Fax 212-213-1539
postmaster@dramatists.com www.dramatists.com

NEW PLAYS

★ **THE CREDEAUX CANVAS by Keith Bunin.** A forged painting leads to tragedy among friends. "There is that moment between adolescence and middle age when being disaffected looks attractive. Witness the enduring appeal of Prince Hamlet, Jake Barnes and James Dean, on the stage, page and screen. Or, more immediately, take a look at the lithe young things in THE CREDEAUX CANVAS..." –*NY Times.* "THE CREDEAUX CANVAS is the third recent play about painters...it turned out to be the best of the lot, better even than most plays about non-painters." –*NY Magazine.* [2M, 2W] ISBN: 0-8222-1838-0

★ **THE DIARY OF ANNE FRANK by Frances Goodrich and Albert Hackett, newly adapted by Wendy Kesselman.** A transcendently powerful new adaptation in which Anne Frank emerges from history a living, lyrical, intensely gifted young girl. "Undeniably moving. It shatters the heart. The evening never lets us forget the inhuman darkness waiting to claim its incandescently human heroine." –*NY Times.* "A sensitive, stirring and thoroughly engaging new adaptation." –*NY Newsday.* "A powerful new version that moves the audience to gasps, then tears." –*A.P.* "One of the year's ten best." – *Time Magazine.* [5M, 5W, 3 extras] ISBN: 0-8222-1718-X

★ **THE BOOK OF LIZ by David Sedaris and Amy Sedaris.** Sister Elizabeth Donderstock makes the cheese balls that support her religious community, but feeling unappreciated among the Squeamish, she decides to try her luck in the outside world. "...[a] delightfully off-key, off-color hymn to clichés we all live by, whether we know it or not." –*NY Times.* "Good-natured, goofy and frequently hilarious..." –*NY Newsday.* "...[THE BOOK OF LIZ] may well be the world's first Amish picaresque...hilarious..." –*Village Voice.* [2M, 2W (doubling, flexible casting to 8M, 7W)] ISBN: 0-8222-1827-5

★ **JAR THE FLOOR by Cheryl L. West.** A quartet of black women spanning four generations makes up this hilarious and heartwarming dramatic comedy. "...a moving and hilarious account of a black family sparring in a Chicago suburb..." –*NY Magazine.* "...heart-to-heart confrontations and surprising revelations...first-rate..." –*NY Daily News.* "...unpretentious good feelings...bubble through West's loving and humorous play..." –*Star-Ledger.* "...one of the wisest plays I've seen in ages...[from] a master playwright." –*USA Today.* [5W] ISBN: 0-8222-1809-7

★ **THIEF RIVER by Lee Blessing.** Love between two men over decades is explored in this incisive portrait of coming to terms with who you are. "Mr. Blessing unspools the plot ingeniously, skipping back and forth in time as the details require...an absorbing evening." –*NY Times.* "...wistful and sweet-spirited..." –*Variety.* [6M] ISBN: 0-8222-1839-9

★ **THE BEGINNING OF AUGUST by Tom Donaghy.** When Jackie's wife abruptly and mysteriously leaves him and their infant daughter, a pungently comic reevaluation of suburban life ensues. "Donaghy holds a cracked mirror up to the contemporary American family, anatomizing its frailties and miscommunications in fractured language that can be both funny and poignant." –*The Philadelphia Inquirer.* "...[A] sharp, eccentric new comedy. Pungently funny...fresh and precise..." –*LA Times.* [3M, 2W] ISBN: 0-8222-1786-4

★ **OUTSTANDING MEN'S MONOLOGUES 2001–2002 and OUTSTANDING WOMEN'S MONOLOGUES 2001–2002 edited by Craig Pospisil.** Drawn exclusively from Dramatists Play Service publications, these collections for actors feature over fifty monologues each and include an enormous range of voices, subject matter and characters. MEN'S ISBN: 0-8222-1821-6 WOMEN'S ISBN: 0-8222-1822-4

DRAMATISTS PLAY SERVICE, INC.
440 Park Avenue South, New York, NY 10016 212-683-8960 Fax 212-213-1539
postmaster@dramatists.com www.dramatists.com